Rejected By Nashville

The Whiskey Rebel

a.k.a.

Phil Irwin

Brilliancy Prize PO Box 1781 San Marcos TX 78666

ISBN-10: 061553564X
ISBN-13: 978-0615535647

DEDICATION

This book is dedicated to my youngest and oldest living relatives. My grandson Hank was born in June of this year. His birth revived my interest in seeing this book through to completion. Also to my beloved hillbilly granny Alma. She hails from Kentucky, but lives today in southern Oregon. Granny has lived out quite a few of the songs praised in this book.

CONTENTS

ACKNOWLEDGMENTS

A tip of the Stetson to Rocco, who was instrumental in shaming me into finally wrapping up this project. My sincere thanks to Kent Finlay, my instructor for a country music history course I completed, at Texas State University (San Marcos). Kent and I disagree taste wise here and there—but I learned much more than I ever expected. Go visit Kent at his club here in San Marcos, The Cheatham Street Warehouse, and tell him the big ugly guy with tattoos says "hi." As usual, thanks to my long, suffering wife Marla, for her technical and editorial work on this book. Cover photographs by Elvis and Sarah Irwin.

INTRODUCTION

Welcome to my take on country music albums. I want to stress right off the bat that music is all a matter of opinion. There is no logical means of evaluating which albums from over the years are great or total garbage. This is my book and my batch of opinions. If any of them disturb you or upset you bear in mind that there are a host of books that line library and bookstore shelves that express all sorts of varying theories concerning country music.

If you are flipping through the pages of this book wondering whether to buy it and want to know where I'm coming from, here's a basic preview of my stance. I prefer what I refer to as real country music, which for many of us is not the stuff trowled out by the current popular Nashville synth-pop industry. Real country does not use sampled drums. Real country is the old fashioned stuff that often features steel and twangy guitars sung frequently by ugly or average looking performers who were the standard for several decades before Nashville began hiring stables of handsome hunks who look good in cowboy hats and belly button waggling gals who look like models.

Can you tell where I'm coming from yet?

Real country music is still performed in all pockets of the USA. The performers rely heavily on the standards set by the pioneers and icons of the genre, ranging from the godfather of country Jimmie Rodgers on down the line to the Carter Family, Ernest Tubb, Hank Williams Sr., Webb Pierce, Kitty Wells, Johnny Cash, Waylon Jennings, Loretta Lynn, Dave Dudley, Red Sovine, Porter Wagoner, Johnny Paycheck, Tammy Wynette, Moe Bandy, Buck Owens, Bill Monroe, Tanya Tucker and Merle Haggard. Included in this guide are many reviews by current performers still faithful to this tradition.

Note! The reviews of CD's by performers still cranking out releases regularly may read as a bit dated. I simply don't have the budget to keep up to the moment on their careers. I'm not on anybody's promo list, so cut me some slack.

Also included are lots of reviews of lesser-known artist's albums from over the years, some of which are extremely obscure, but deserving of attention in my view.

There are sections of reviews devoted to certain sub-genres of country music that fit under the tent shall we say: "Truck driving", "Honky Tonk", "Duet", etc.

My pet peeves will surely effect your enjoyment of this book. I'm a sucker for drinking and cheating songs; if you consider those sorts of tunes wicked, you probably had best put this back on the shelf and seek out a tame encyclopedia of C&W, there are many to choose from.

I have little use for what Rolling Stone magazine and other publications have referred to for many years as "country rock," yunno, Gram Parsons, America, the Eagles, Poco, etc. Besides my occasional ranting against these artists within the reviews, I've included facts and dates that further my claim that plenty of other artists who are routinely ignored by the rock music press combined elements of rock and roll and country music well before the hippie generation performers they glorify. False heroes are wearing the laurels, hence my gettin' pissed off here and there.

I started out buying country LPs at thrift stores about 30 years ago. I own every album reviewed in these pages and rarely paid more than $1 for them. This is very much a fan book written for folks on a budget. You can still find tons of real country albums at flea markets and record shows and yard sales for that same $1 or under.

I realized years ago when I was planning out this book, that you're never gonna find some great music by certain old timers on vinyl without shelling out some big bucks. Many of the albums included in these pages by ancient pioneers such as Grandpa Jones are indeed CDs. I've pointed this out in several cases within the pages.

Most of the music by current musicians is of course from CDs. The most important thing is to have the music one way or another; if you're loyal to one format you're limiting yourself. Hell, if you have an old 8-track player, put it to use. You can go hit the flea markets and load up on vintage 8-tracks of many albums I've reviewed for dirt-cheap.

I like to drink cheap beer and whiskey when I listen to country music. I'm comfortable at blue-collar taverns watching one of the current aficionados of country at work. At such times I might get wild or even borderline rowdy.

The fact is though, this book was written and edited 100% er, uh well 98% sober. A helluva lot of serious work went into this. Even though I quickly discarded the notion of using footnotes (there are plenty of footnoted country history books out there) I've included a bibliography. I graduated a few years ago from Texas State University cum laude with a History degree and an English minor. I've read up heavily on the subject at hand and even completed a senior undergrad level History course on country music history. I had already written an early version of this book and was ready to test my knowledge. What's that? Yep, I earned an "A."

One more thing; the sections are simple groupings I casually created in the final stages of the layout of this book. Originally, I had assigned numbers ranking about 240 of the albums in order from best to worst (you will find a longer discussion about this in the epilogue). Some artists are seen in more than one list. Don't lose any sleep over your favorite singer being in a section you wouldn't have chosen. I don't like categorizing music, but felt the book needed some sort of structure.

The *Keepers of the Flame* section was designed to group together some great talents who are in the prime of their careers, recording real country music. My purpose is not to imply that folks covered somewhere else in these pages who are still playing somewhere are over the hill. I know George Jones and Willie Nelson for instance are still performing; I consider them rather than keepers of the flame, to be amongst the icons that lit it in the first place. OK?

Phil Irwin

August 16, 2011

San Marcos, Texas

1. BLUEGRASS

BILL MONROE “Greatest Hits” MCA. LP

I was lucky enough to see Bill Monroe play live once. It just happened to be the very first time I attended a bluegrass concert. I was amazed to see the crazy quilt of people who turned out. There were entire families of folks dressed in their Sunday best sporting conservative long dresses, suits and ties and slicked back hair. I also saw a lot of guys wearing Western type clothing complete with hats and tie bolos. There was also a sizable contingent of hippie types clad in tie-dye T-shirts, earth-shoes, etc. There were even a smattering of punk rock types here and there looking a bit nervous and out of place.

I didn’t know it at the time, but that was a fairly normal bluegrass concert audience. The beauty, energy and honesty of the music of the king of bluegrass, Bill Monroe is timeless. It’s aged over the years as gracefully as Coca-Cola.

This album is just one of many great collections made available over the years loaded with consistently great songs such as "Molly and Tenbrooks" "New Mule Skinner Blues" and "Uncle Pen" plus instrumentals "Cheyenne" and "Roanoke" etc.

Enough can't be said about the significance of Mr. Monroe's place in American musical history for spearheading in his generation a genre of music that has one foot rooted in the past, yet is as popular on a grass roots basis as it possibly ever has been. It's satisfying for an alienated guy like me who loathes most popular culture to know that bluegrass music will still be around and thriving when the trendy music of today is dead and buried.

FLATT & SCRUGGS "Greatest Hits" (1960's) Columbia Records. LP.

These icons of bluegrass were a class act without a doubt. Their smooth but spirited picking blended perfectly with their easygoing, good-natured vocal tracks. Several impressive instrumental numbers are included here including "Earl's Breakdown" "Fireball" and "Flint Hill Special." As a special treat a trio of TV related songs are featured: "The Ballad of Jed Clampett" (which needs no introduction) "Pearl Pearl Pearl" which also stems from the Beverly Hillbillies show (Pearl was Jethro's Ma, Jed's sis) and the theme from "Petticoat Junction." I for one wish they had tackled the "Green Acres" theme while they were at it, but what the hell. These songs are all rural as hell compared to the rock and roll songs of the day that were considered so much more sophisticated. But even "hick" tunes such as "My Saro Jane" and the Carter family standard "Jimmy Brown the Newsboy" seem to have stood the test of time much better than a huge chunk of the trendier rock and roll hits of the '60's. I offer as evidence the fact that new bluegrass combos made up of young players are thriving in many parts of the country. I've never ever heard a band of young people playing exclusively top-40 mainstream '60's pop hits. So, no matter that hipsters considered them corny back in the day, Flatt and Scruggs buried '60's pop music.

GEEZINSLAW BROTHERS "Can you Believe" (1966) Capitol. LP

Hailing from Snook Texas, the Geezinslaw's (not their real names) combined some of the best elements of more famous duo's Homer and Jethro and Flatt and Scruggs. One picked mandolin, the other guit-fiddle. One looked like TV'S Drew Carey and the other like a guy who sells cemetery plots. They picked very well and Capitol obviously spared no expense at providing great novelty material for these fellas.

The album kicks off with a salute to their hometown "Snook is the Only Town For Me" penned by Ned and Sue Miller. The infamous Lee Hazelwood contributed "They Called him Country" and "Four Kinds of Lonely." Both tunes have a nutty edge that the Geezinslaws pull off quite well. The listener can soon recognize a definite Geezinslaw style at work in these songs. The boys are funny, yet they hold back from Smothers-like hilarity, and the social commentary is kept light and simple. This is one of those rare solid albums you can let both sides play through rather than keep excusing yourself from company to skip past the duds causing them to cover their ears and drool on the floor.

HOMER & JETHRO "At the Country Club" (1960) LP.

For a quarter century or so guitarist Homer Haynes and mandolin picker Jethro Burns were the music world's undisputed song parody geniuses. Not long ago I read an interview with X-rated R&B song parody King Blowfly; when asked how he was influenced to embark on a career of poking fun of song hits he told the interviewer about hearing Homer and Jethro on the radio when he was a child. I'd bet my last quart of beer Weird Al Yankovic was directly inspired by them too. To be honest though, Homer and Jethro merely commercialized what folks everywhere have been doing since the advent of long road trips and beer chug-a-lugs.

I've read anecdotes about Hank Williams and his boys driving from town to town crafting nasty versions of his classic songs while passing the bottle. Elvis Presley not only sat around the piano goofing on songs with his pals backstage, he'd bust out into alternate lyrics on stage whenever he felt like it. Ditto for Dean Martin. His biographer Nick Tosches relates that towards the end of his career Dino wouldn't sing even one complete song in his live set without changing the words around into something funny or smutty.

This live album is a fine representation of what Homer and Jethro were all about. They poke fun at Elvis with "Hart Brake Motel." They manage to squeeze laughs out of the very serious Tennessee Ernie Ford anthem "Sixteen Tons." They even dismantle one of the Lone Star state's most hallowed songs "Yaller Rose of Texas." In between songs the boys crack corny jokes putting each other down. They weren't a cocky and mean spirited act. Back in the day only an asshole would have been less than thrilled to have Homer and Jethro record a version of their song. I'd give anything to know the inside story on which sensitive artists were upset at being parodied and which laughed the hardest.

Homer and Jethro's studio albums are all classics too. I'm waving the banner for this one though since you get to hear their entire act of jokes and songs together.

HOMER and JETHRO "The Far out World of" (1972) RCA. LP.

According to my trusty record guide this album is at the end of the long, long string of albums recorded by this duo. The back cover liner notes are written by Jethro Burns. He reminds us that Homer passed away in August of 1971 and pays tribute to him in an appropriately irreverent manner. Compared to the other dozen or so albums of theirs I have, several of these songs seem to be pushing the limits a bit which makes me wonder if they were held back for the sad day of the demise of the duo.

"Act Naturally" ala Homer and Jethro has become a genuine anti-Vietnam war song declaring that it's better to be sentenced to a stockade than die in a jungle. That's a brave attitude to have taken in the face of the conservative country music audience of the early '70's. The "Girl From Possum Holler" (which I find hilarious) would result in feminist picket lines if released today. "Daddy Played First Base" pokes fun of a Carl Perkin's hymn that my mother loves. "We Didn't Make it Through the Night" butchers Kris Kristofferson's hit. These guys started out in 1946 and they went out with a bang rather than a whimper with this standout album.

PLUM HOLLOW BAND s/t . Plum Hollow Records. LP

Led by Barney Barnwell this outfit has been playing its brand of rowdy style bluegrass all over the south for a long time. This album dates back to the early '80's but they're going at it stronger than ever as of this writing. Since I was added to their email list I've learned that Barney has built on his 50 acre property a sophisticated outdoor stage set up complete with restroom and shower facilities to deal with several thousand music lovers at a time. Damn, I admire the "do it yourself" ethic on the part of musicians. I also admire that these boys don't apologize for their southern heritage.

They kick off the album with two numbers that let you know where they stand right off: a "Dixie Medley" and the moonshine anthem "Run Grandpa Run." I love the variety of this album. Sometimes they settle into a pretty picking mode and other times they crank up the attitude with originals like "Hippie Song" and "'Be No Beer Joints in Heaven." I can tell from their website that over the years they've grown like any other good band. This was a helluva way to start out. I suggest you track down this album pronto (I think it's available as a CD now). If we had a few dozen more bands across America with Barney and Plum Hollow's initiative the Nashville music business could just fold up its tents.

STRINGBEAN Front Porch Funnies" King label. CD

Poor Stringbean; cut down in his prime by moronic murderous thugs. Every time I listen to this I knock back a shot in his honor. Yunno, I'm not sure the year of these recordings, but with Stringbean that doesn't matter so much considering how his singin' and banjo pickin' is timeless. I bet String and his neighbor and Fred and Barney type pal, Grandpa Jones and he used to sit on the porch sometimes and just blaze away at some of these songs they both played on stage for years and years such as, "How Many Biscuits Can you Eat?" and "Mountain Dew." I get a big kick out of "Chewing Gum" and "Run Rabbit Run" which is a sort of hunting song that's sympathetic to the poor little bunny. Remember the Beverly Hillbillies episode in which Jethro told a gaggle of hippies he was hanging out with: "My Granny Smokes Crawdads!" The hippies were confused. Impressed, but confused. The lyrics to "I'm the Man That Road the Mule Around the World" tickles my fancy in the same way.

Oh yeah. A reminder to the fashion conscious: Stringbean invented those droopy ass crack exposing hip hop style trousers 30 years before they became popular. There's a picture of him wearing them on the back cover of this CD.

2. CASH

JOHNNY CASH "At FOLSOM PRISON" Columbia Records. LP.

If you ever wonder just why Johnny Cash has been elevated by society in general (not just country music fans) to the amazing level of respect he receives, here's a damn good audio explanation. Obviously on the day this was recorded Cash was under pressure to deliver the goods technically speaking so this album could offset Columbia Record's obviously high recording costs. It seems like Johnny probably planned things out the best he could before he took the stage in front of the 2,000 convicts. From the get-go Johnny is obviously totally devoted to pleasing the "captive" audience of prisoners. There are a few technical flaws here and there, but so what. Johnny probably didn't give a damn by that point. When you've got a mob of inmates screaming and eating out of your hand, so what if there's a fucking glitch or blown note here or there. Some songs are about as perfect as they ever will be performed in this lifetime "Folsom Prison Blues" "Cocaine Blues" and "25 Minutes to Go" for instance. When June comes onstage for "Jackson" the audience begins to pant and crackle and sound almost inhuman. Those boys appreciate seeing any woman and Ms. June was quite a looker. By the time "Green Green Grass of Home" is sung it doesn't matter that Cash can't compete with Tom Jones or Porter Wagoner when it comes to crooning it. It's sung purely for the boys in the audience. It's no wonder Cash is probably deified by more plain folk of all races in the USA than anybody else. Brooks may have sold more units, but when he goes it won't be a pimple on the ass of the world's reaction when Johnny went. Mark my words.

JOHHNY CASH "At San Quentin" (1960's) Columbia Records. LP.

Even though this album and Johnny's "Live at Folsom Prison" album were both huge commercial successes, there didn't seem to be a huge rush by labels and country music performers to try to cash in on this sort of album. That's probably due to the fact that most other performers would simply have a helluva time trying to connect with the prisoners. A few others come to mind but they never succeeded like Cash. As Johnny relates in his song included here "Starkville Country Jail" he never spent serious time behind bars, but for some reason he obviously had a knack for talking to the boys in pinstripes. The opening number chosen is perfect "Wanted Man" by Bob Dylan. The pinnacle of this five star album is the two back-to-back versions (loudly demanded by the convicts in attendance) of "San Quentin" which seem almost shockingly critical of the prison to be performed in full view of the prison warden and his staff. Cash immediately swings straight into a relatively lighthearted number (and billion selling single I might add) "A Boy Named Sue" perhaps to cool the mood down a bit. The final song as might have been expected is "Folsom Prison Blues" which makes the convicts scream so loud I wonder how in the hell the poor Statler Brothers (whom Johnny announces would be on next) ever managed to follow this set?

JOHNNY CASH "Look at them Beans"(1975) Columbia Records. LP.

Mr. Cash of course recorded as wide a variety of albums as any man who ever walked into a recording studio. Love songs, train songs, violent songs recorded in prisons, gospel, you name it. This album shows Johnny's family man side. "No Charge" is as down home as Red Sovine singing with his granddaughters. "Look at Them Beans" is flat-out rural. I think it's a great song though the way it builds and builds from being somber to pure unbridled joy. "I Hardly Ever Sing Beer-Drinking Songs" is a Cash penned tune that comes right out and admits that he may sound like a bit of a square to some folks with the songs he's singing. It's a funny song, not judgmental in the least. It reflects the mood of this batch of mid '70's tunes.

"Down at Dripping Springs" is a salute from a distance to the outlaw scene going down in Texas at the time. It's plain though at this time in his life Johnny Cash was focused on his flesh and blood family as opposed to some of his hell raising buddies. Domesticated or not, these are Johnny Cash songs and they are good. They have their place, although I'd play the Folsom prison album at my Saturday night beer bust and save this for Sunday afternoon.

JOHNNY CASH "Mean as Hell" (1965) Columbia Records. LP.

The subtitle to this album is "Ballads from the True West" and the back cover liner notes describe the sometimes-dangerous lengths Johnny went to in order to experience first hand the "Wild, Hot and Unbelievable" American West. "The Shifting Whispering Sands Pt. 1" followed by "I Ride an Old Paint" and "The Road to Kaintuck", get us started down the trail in a pleasant enough mood. But soon the mood darkens and the trail gets a bit rougher while Johnny sings "Mean As Hell." We reach the pinnacle of this album Shel Silversteins hangin' song "25 Minutes to Go" which is merely one of the most unforgettable tunes ever recorded in any genre.

The mood rarely lightens up much on side two. "The Blizzard" is as tragic a love song that you're gonna hear. "Stampede" and "Bury Me Not on the Lone Prairie" wrap this album up; a mostly melancholy collection of numbers meant to depict the true historical west as opposed to the happy ending stories so popular on television during the mid '60's. This album is just further proof of Johnny Cash's great knack for producing a wide variety of albums as opposed to so many of his contemporaries who seemed to record the same album of love songs over and over. Mr. Cash declared in his autobiography that he's a real history buff, a hobby that obviously came in useful designing the course of this LP, which is truly great for what it is.

JOHNNY CASH "Ride this Train" (1959) Columbia Records. LP.

Another innovative and unique album from the man in black. These are Western songs, stitched together by both railroad sounds and Johnny's educational but never dry or dull narrations. After a quick verse or two naming Indian tribes and place names (similar to "I've Been Everywhere") our first stop is Kentucky's coal country (where my own maternal grandmother hails from--whom this book is co-dedicated to). "Loading Coal" speaks of a tough but honest existence. A couple stops later we're in southern Oregon (where Granny lives to this day) where we're treated to "Lumberjack" which ranks up there with even Buzz Martin's best songs about logging. On side two, Johnny's "Goin' to Memphis" before making a detour to South Carolina to sing "When Papa Played the dobro." "Boss Jack" is an interesting number set in pre-civil war Arkansas and sung from the viewpoint of a slave with an enlightened owner who is kind to him. A fine trip that never bogs down at any of the stops.

JOHNNY CASH "Ring of Fire" (1963) Columbia Records. LP.

A potluck of different types of Cash songs, we've got all time great hits like the title tune; "Ring of Fire", "I Still Miss Someone" and "Tennessee Flat-top Box". Two Western TV show themes are sung to spine tingling effect "Bonanza" and "The Rebel Johnny Yuma". Then there're two that reflect Mr. Cash's yen for historical songs "The Big Battle" "Remember the Alamo" and a pair of side ending gospel numbers with June and the rest of the current Carters joining in "Peace In the Valley" and "Were You There."

Of course even though Johnny Cash seems godlike and larger than life to so many folks, he pulls all these songs off just being himself. He'd be the first to tell you that. Minimalist guitarist Luther Perkins has several outstanding moments on this album, which he pulls off with great ease and class. Cash and the Tennessee Two are as usual simple and natural as twist top bottles. The elaborate, overwrought and often pretentious musical pap heard on commercial country radio these days hasn't improved upon the purity of this trio. These Cash songs will still sound great 100 years from now. Today's TRENDY, CONTRIVED SHIT will simply be replaced by Tomorrow's TRENDY, CONTRIVED SHIT and be forgotten.

JOHNNY CASH "The Baron" (1981) Columbia Records. LP.

Twenty-three years on with Columbia Records by the time this album was recorded and Johnny Cash was still capable of packing an LP with great songs. Some fine story telling here, my favorite being a tale of the hitchhike-ride-from-hell "Chattanooga City Limit Sign" written by "B. Drawdy" I would've bet all the money in my wallet it was a Shel Silverstein song when I first heard it. The recitation "Mobile Bay" and Tom T. Hall's "A Ceiling Four Walls and a Floor" are both moving songs that fit Mr. Cash's voice perfectly. For that matter "The Baron" and "The Reverend Mr. Black" hold me on the edge of my seat too. "Thanks To You" is the song I for one have always wanted to hear thanking a former now out of the picture main squeeze for the songs she's inspired. Produced by Billy Sherrill, yet another classic Johnny Cash album. No sign here of why

Columbia Records should've felt compelled to dump and reject him a year or two later.

JOHNNY CASH "The World of" Columbia Records. Two LP collection.

I have about a jillion Johnny Cash albums. I'm positive even he couldn't tell you how many slabs of vinyl he appeared on, spanning his days with the Sun label, up through his very long association with Columbia. Of course recording artists rarely can. It's their business to create great music, not to gawk like a geek at every individual release the record company issues with their name on it. Which leaves me wondering how big a shelf you'd need to store one of each of every variation of every release he's appeared on the world over.

I bet I must have 20 albums at least with "Folsom Prison Blues" on it. That's great for the folks who want to hear Johnny's best-loved songs, but it's a bit difficult to find a lot of his lesser-known songs that don't regularly make it to the reissue packages. This two album is perfect to seek out if you want to expand your Cash collection without getting yet another pressing of the same songs you already have. There are a handful of train songs including the dramatic "The Legend of John Henry's Hammer" and "Casey Jones."

Old country favorites such as; "I Forgot More Than You'll Ever Know" and "My Shoes Keep Walking Back to You." There are rural roots themed songs included that never make the greatest hits albums "Supper Time", "Pickin' Time" and "In Them Old Cotton fields Back Home." I think most Cash fans would find it worth a couple long hard days in the cotton fields to find a copy of this. This "sack" holds

20 tunes and there are no rocks (filler material) in the bottom of the bag.

JOHNNY CASH "Unchained" (1996) American Recordings. CD.

Let's face it, who else but Johnny Cash from his generation could pull off damn good versions of songs by comparative youngsters like Beck and Soundgarden? I'll tell you what; I didn't believe he could make songs by those folks sound like anything I'd want to hear a second time until I heard it for myself. Yep. Forty years into his career and the man in black wasn't about to coast along a safe road re-recording old hits for nostalgic old fans. This album shows him in timeless and fearless form for sure. Just a few days ago my son taped songs off of this disc for his 16-year-old band mate. What does that tell you?

You can let this CD play straight through it's pretty solid. Johnny's voice hadn't slipped a bit here even though he recorded this at an age when many acclaimed senior citizen golden throats (such as Frank Sinatra) have been torn to pieces by the cruel critics. The songs that really tickle my fancy are "Sea of Heartbreak" "Country Boy" and a string of inspired covers "Memories Are Made of This" "I Never Picked Cotton" and the dynamite version of Hank Snow's "I've Been Everywhere."

I'm not a huge fan of the backup band Tom Petty's Heartbreakers (Ok, ok... I'm not a fan of theirs at all) but I've got to credit them for a fine, tasteful job working for Mr. Cash. They sound like a solid living breathing band as opposed to all the boring, sampled, over-produced horseshit. Bravo.

3. DUETS

GEORGE JONES & TAMMY WYNETTE "The President and the First Lady" (1981) Cindy Lou's Musical Mail Order/CBS. LP.

This 20-song disc features enough great tunes to provide further proof (along with lots of other blue ribbon winners in this book) that TV albums aren't to be sneered at. Side one starts off with "We're Gonna Hold On" an inspiring tune that George admitted in his autobiography was purely meant to capitalize on the fact that George & Tammy fans wanted to believe they'd magically repaired their marriage which fell apart years and years before the publicity wing of their record label would ever admit. "The Ceremony" complete with spoken word vows and a priest makes me grin every time. I hear it was a highlight of their live set also long after they called it quits romantically. "We're Not the Jet Set" begins with a few lines spoofing that the Jones's were highbrow snobs hanging out in snooty European cities. It's a grassroots anthem for ordinary country music fan couples. One after another various angles of couples either falling apart, coming together or just hanging in there are explored in this collection. "Southern California" "Golden Ring" and "God's Gonna Getcha for That" are a few more of my favorites. There's not a clinker to be found within. These are two of the very best singers of all time and they had every yahoo at every damned guitar pull in Nashville bending over backwards to write songs tailored for them to use. No wonder this is so damned good.

GEORGE JONES & JOHNNY PAYCHECK "Double Trouble" (1980) Epic Records. LP.

Two of the greatest all time masters of slow and intense honky tonk songs and what do we get? What did they churn out? A batch of rock and roll oldies. Oh what the hell. I'd pay to hear these two sing the damned phonebook as they say.

Chuck Berry's "Maybelline" and "Roll Over Beethoven" are both well arranged and sung. There's a helluva blistering guitar player weaving in and out playing Jerry Reed type licks. The Coaster's classic "Along Came Jones" and Wilbert Harrison's "Kansas City" have been re-arranged from their original R&B sounds to a sort of redneck strut. George and Johnny laugh their way through the session for the most part especially the lead off song "When You're Ugly Like Us (You Just Naturally Got to Be Cool)" and "You Can Have Her."

It's anybody's guess why they wound up singing these sorts of songs rather than double-teaming some songs of misery, but what the hell. It's not like these guys haven't both recorded a lot of novelty and rock and roll numbers in the past. The more I ponder on it, It seems perfectly natural that when a couple old buddies like these two get together they're not gonna sing sad songs to each other.

When Sam Phillips "Million Dollar Quartet" magically congregated around the piano at Sun studios in the mid-1950's they didn't start banging out rockabilly or dirty blues they sang gospel songs to the enduring disappointment of a few generations of rock and roll fans.

It's no different with Jones and Paycheck; when they get together they're gonna sing what the hell they want to sing.

HANK SNOW and ANITA CARTER "Together Again" (1962) RCA. LP.

I was lucky enough to read about this album in Johnny Cash's autobiography a few days before I happened to spot a copy at a used record store. He wrote a bit about a pact that the Carter sisters made at one point concerning recording only as a group. He contends that the world was worse off for not having a slew of albums to listen to sung by his sister-in-law Anita Carter, whom he praised as being one of the finest female country singers of all time. I immediately thought of the audio version of a TV appearance by her in which Hank Sr. comes up from behind her as a surprise to duet with her; it's included on Hanks late '90's CD box set. I don't have a clue how Hank Snow managed to get sis Anita into the studio but I'm glad he did. Johnny's right. She's got a voice that's prettier than a bug's ear. The songs chosen and the sparse but pretty arrangements take this LP in a dignified folk direction as opposed to a slew of "funny-fight" songs that so many country duos have had commercial hits with. The standard

"Mockin' Bird Hill" has in all likelihood never been sung better on vinyl. The Carter Family standard "I Never Will Marry" is an impressive nod towards Anita's kin folk and a fine indicator of what sort of career Anita could have achieved working on her own more often, definitely an album worth seeking out in any format.

MERLE HAGGARD & BONNIE OWENS "Just Between the Two of Us" (1966) Capitol Records. LP.

As of this writing, Bonnie Owens (formerly Mrs. Buck Owens and briefly Mrs. Haggard) is still singing with Merle on tour. When I saw his road show several years ago she sang lead on a song and brought down the damned house. When the material on this album was recorded in the mid '60's Merle was relatively green and hadn't yet risen to the living legend status that he enjoys now. Frankly, Merle sounds quite a bit like Buck here at times, not that there's anything wrong with that. His voice is high pitched throughout most of the album never really venturing into middle or lower register as he has most of his career.

Bonnie's voice is rustic and deep-hick compared to the Dottie West's and Connie Smith's of country music. I prefer her voice to theirs by a long shot. Taken together Merle and Bonnie's vocals are beautiful and rich. Both vocals are so peachy my ear doesn't know which to follow. The musical arrangements here are 100% Bakersfield, complete with twangy guitars and borderline rock and roll beats. The songs chosen are almost all from the "fragile relationship" category. Standouts are Hank Sr.'s "A House Without Love is Not a Home" Buck's "Forever and Ever", "Stranger In My Arms" (penned by producer Fuzzy Owens) and Liz

Anderson's "So Much For Me So Much For You." Considering the fact that these two are still possibly out on the road singing together, this album's gotta be considered an important milestone in the history of west coast style country.

MERLE HAGGARD & GEORGE JONES "Yesterdays Wine" (1982) Epic Records. LP.

Wow! Imagine the line of Nashville songwriters queuing up at the bar at Tootsie's in search of an Epic Records scout to try to get their songs onto this one. In the end it was Merle himself who penned the biggest hit from this meeting of these titans "C.C. Waterback" that begins with a story about these two partying one night at the Jones place (possibly based upon fact) and winds up touting an alcoholic dandy hangover cure. Willie Nelson of course penned the title track. It's sung so naturally by these two that you'd have thunk it was written with them in mind. So does "Must've Been Drunk" by the mighty Vern Gosdin and Leona Williams Haggard's "After I Sing All My Songs" which is all about the backstage post concert needs of superstars like these guys. George gets the last word on the album with his self-parody, "No Show Jones."

Needless to say, this album is as welcome as the roses in May whether or not George remembers much of what went on in the studio. Billy Sherrill was at the helm behind the board to watch his back and with that kind of proven quality production help you can go ahead and get shitfaced knowing you're gonna enjoy the results the next day.

MOE BANDY & JOE STAMPLEY "Hey Joe Hey Moe" (1981) Columbia Records. LP.

These boys sure as hell have proven themselves individually as capable singers of "serious" (I hate that word) songs. This album and a couple that followed it is a chance for these guys to have fun and sing about the finer things in life: beer, pickin', beer, telling off snobs that hate country music, beer, dancing in taverns, beer... you get the idea.

"Honky Tonk Queen" is a hilarious slab of cross-dressing humor. "Two Beers Away" is a vital hangover cure number that amateurs should pay close attention to. "Get Off My Case" is a double upraised finger towards assholes who are always putting down good 'ol beer drinking 'necks and their music. "Let's Hear it for the Workin' Man" is a natural bottoms-up blue-collar anthem that'll leave you trotting to the cooler for more fresh cans.

Do I need to add how much this album must burn up all the highbrow intellectual snots that loathe these sorts of pleasures that Moe, Joe and I enjoy so much? As far as I'm concerned, anybody that'd look down his or her nose at Moe Bandy and Joe Stampley deserves to have it bloodied. While we're at it, my idea of "diversity" is buying Bud one night and Coors the next.

4. THE GALS

CONNIE SMITH s/t (1965) RCA. LP.

Bill Anderson discovered Connie, brought her to RCA and penned six songs for this debut LP. The backing band is all crackerjack players. Label honcho Chet Atkins must've felt in his bones right off how durable a talent he was dealing with. Just like some country music singers have a niche be it novelty songs, outlaw stance tunes, etc., Connie's niche is relationship songs, not too violent or steamy. Her voice is too pretty to warrant her bellowing or coming across as a badass babe. Loretta and Kitty both sounded at times like they could knock cheeteroo hubbie's teeth down his throat; not so Connie. She comes across as the forgiving type. "Once a Day" was the big hit on this album. I'm partial to the cleverly written "I'm Ashamed of You" "The Hinges on the Door" and the truly woe some "Darling Are You Ever Coming Home?"

DOTTIE WEST "The Sound of Country Music" (1967) RCA. LP.

What a set of ..uhh.. lungs! Seriously. When Dottie starts off this album with Loretta Lynn's "You Aint Woman Enough" she doesn't sound like she'd whip Loretta in a cat fight, but she could sure dish it out at well as any other gal when it came to vocalizing. I like the way that she's backed very simply on this album by a small combo as opposed to the more lavish arrangements that accompanied her later in her career. Her quality voice carries my attention.

I don't need to hear a violin section to appreciate her talents. She sings several "memorable" (record company liner note jargon for "often covered") songs such as "Pick Me Up On Your Way Down" "Heartaches By the Number" and a tune literally every other RCA artist of the '60's seems to have covered "Crazy Arms." Dottie must've seemed like a red-hot up and coming label property at this point in time in spite of the matronly gown and frumpy hair-do she's sporting on the cover. I'm glad she went sexpot image wise later on, but I'll take this small honky tonk backup band any day over the pop crossover orchestra's she sang with down the road.

JEAN SHEPARD "Many Happy Hangovers" (mid 60's) Capitol LP.

A lot of female country singers over the years have sung meek songs of subservience to men-folk. This album is refreshingly different. Jean Shepard instead flips the bird at her no good man wishing the agony of regular hangovers at him. The album cover asserts the undisputable fact that Ms. Shepard was a hot looking blonde. Any knucklehead who'd dally with her affections must be a moron. She maintains a pissed off attitude with Harlan Howard's "I Forgot To Care" "Wave Goodbye to Me" and the blunt "Dirt Under My Feet." Most of the album sustains the mood. There are certainly no humble apology songs to be found.

I rarely see copies of this album in the usual thrift stores and flea markets I regularly plunder for country LPs. It must not have sold too well. That's a shame. The feisty attitude must have been a few years ahead of its time.

KITTY WELLS "Showcase" Decca Records. LP

Before Tammy, before Loretta, before Patsy country music fans had Kitty Wells. Yeah, she may have come along after Maybelle Carter and some others, but when she arrived on the scene in 1950, there weren't many women putting butts in the seats as they say. Her success elevated her beyond the billing status of a typical show opening girl singer and paved the way for other gals to follow.

In these days of diva country/pop/R&B crossover female singers I suppose Kitty Wells might seem pretty square given the fact that she never displayed cleavage on her record covers. Rubbish! She simply let her voice represent her. This collection of songs which was released in the late 1960's wasn't marketed to the flower loving hippies in Berkeley; there are no photos of Kitty cramming herself into hip hugger pants or sporting a bleached blonde look. The art on the cover shows Kitty wearing a conservative style purple western dress. Maybe she doesn't look hot by contemporary Howard Stern show standards, but at the truck stops and small-town record shops from sea to shining sea she sold a damned helluva lot of units being herself.

The leadoff track is "My Big Truck Drivin' Man" which is a sentimental female answer of sorts to all the male crooned truck driving songs from the era. "Burning a Hole In My Mind" "You Want Her Not Me" and Harlan Howard's "The Chokin'Kind" are three classic "psychological" country songs Kitty interprets in a folksy but thoughtful manor. Hell, she's miles beyond the moon/June/spoon female pop dreck of the day. Kitty Well's voice is like a good truck stop chicken fried steak that you don't realize until a year later was the best meal you've had in years.

LIZ ANDERSON "Husband Hunting" (1970) RCA. LP.

A lot of pop albums from 1970 or so feature too many "cause oriented" songs for my liking. That's not the case with this record thankfully. Liz Anderson is in fine form here with a set of good ol' traditional country music songs. The title track "Husband Hunting" (one of a few written by Liz) has a sort of ironic twist in another direction from what the album cover would lead you to expect. It's fun to hear a female sing "Okie From Muskogee." Over the years there's been a great deal of debate of course as to where Merle's head was at when he recorded it. Liz handles all of the topical lines in stride. I like her version of the old chestnut "Born to Lose" too. Another fine Liz song included is "Don't Leave the Leaving Up to Me." She makes the most of contemporary hit "Down In the Boondocks" although I bet one of the producers brought the song to the session. Thankfully they didn't try to talk her into wearing hippie clothes on the cover to be "fashionable."

LORETTA LYNN "Don't Come Home a Drinkin'" (1967) Decca. LP.

The title song has got to be some sort of cultural milestone; up until this point, women rarely sassed back at their men folk within the confines of a country music song. Although she's better known for other songs, if I could only play one Loretta Lynn number to represent her to some curious life form from outer space this would be the one. By 1967 the world of country music had quite enough songs sung by females reflecting a grin and bear it attitude when it came to their big, drunk, smelly men coming and going as they pleased, expecting the little lady to "put out" when they waltz in home from a drunken spree at 4:00 a.m.

In real life many fellers have received knots in the head from flying rolling pins or frying pans when coming home like that. Take it from me. I've been married 25 plus years. You don't come home after closing up the honkytonks and start pawing all over yer slumbering wife or drag her by the hair into the kitchen to cook you a meal unless you are very confused or have a death wish. You only get away with that sort of shit in Erskine Caldwell books written several decades ago or in rural movies such as Deliverance.

"Get What 'cha Got And Go," is another real life tune from this album the meaning of which you can figure out from the title unless you're a total nitwit. "The Shoe Goes On the Other Foot Tonight" is a punishment that's dished out to thousands of men from coast to coast every week by women who sneer at that stand by your man song.

The final tune is a rather un-apologetic number titled "I Got Caught." Loretta flat out shrugs it off. Her attitude is: so what? Up yers buddy! Some people may think it's a miracle Loretta and her husband Doolittle stayed together for many, many years. She clearly got a lot of ideas for songs out of his trifling.

NORMA JEAN "I Guess that Comes from Being Poor" (1972) RCA. LP.

A theme album of poverty, and humble origins songs, there's a few similarities you might expect between this album and some of Norma's former employer Porter Wagoner's tragic concept LPs. The arrangement of "Hundred Dollar Funeral" is very close to that of Porter's version. As on many of his LPs, a Dolly Parton song is included "Coat of Many Colors." The song selection is very Porter-ish. Did he produce this but not want his name on it so as to help promote Norma Jean's "post-Porter" solo career?

I dunno. She's got a fine homey voice that I don't get tired of. "One on the Way" is a great novelty song delivered perfectly and "Po Folks" and "I Guess That Comes From Being Poor" are solid, poor but proud anthems.

Oddly enough, in spite of any Porter involvement or influence me thinks it's more likely to please Loretta's fans than Dottie's.

PATSY CLINE "Greatest Hits" MCA Records. LP.

The eternal all-time jukebox mega-classics included here "Walking After Midnight" "Crazy" "I Fall to Pieces" and "Sweet Dreams" simply never seem to lose their appeal. To this day, it's just as likely you'll hear these songs playing at an urban hipster bar as a backwoods dive. The songs are topnotch, handpicked from some of the best songwriters of the day. Patsy's voice is just right at all times not too hick, not too citified.

This very night as I write this I happened to hear an interview on the radio with one of the biggest selling female "country" (HAH!) singers of today. She was asked who her main influences were. Even though her music has all the personality of a paint commercial, she immediately named Patsy Cline. It may actually be true that this label creation has musical influences. It may even be true that she's heard Patsy. Of course, it may also be true that's she's simply been coached to answer "Patsy Cline" whenever she's asked that question. If so it's plain to understand why the publicity folks from her label would want her to claim to be enamored with Pasty Cline, an icon whose top records to this day hang in there with the biggest platters Elvis and Frank and Hank ever recorded, not to mention Garth and Shania. For Christ's sake, even the most sour pussed gaggle of old ladies I've ever worked alongside loved Patsy's classics and they hated music.

RUBY WRIGHT "Dern Ya" (1966) Kapp Records. LP

I bet you didn't even know that Kitty Wells has a daughter. Yep, it's Ruby. Her old man must've been Johnnie Wright of "Johnnie and Jack" fame. This LP owes a lot more to Roger Miller than to Ma or Pa's styles though. The title track answer tune to Miller's "Dang Me" is only the first of a slew of funny songs. "Billy Broke My Heart At Walgreen's" is a tongue in cheek novelty teen heartache song the likes of which isn't recorded in Nashville any more unfortunately. "Smarty Britches" is a feisty number about a country boy who's been to the city and comes home with a swelled head that reminds me of the old Barney Fife return to Mayberry, Andy Griffith episode. There are some well sung non novelty tunes here including the "Gay Divorcee" (they'd have to change that title these days) and "Once a Day" which is a pretty post breakup number penned by Bill Anderson. I don't think that Ruby had a very long recording career according to my record guides. That's a shame. Great songs. Fine voice. I rate this album right up there along side the best work of the better-known gal singers of the '60's.

SKEETER DAVIS "Sings Buddy Holly" (1967) RCA Records. LP.

"Tribute" albums rarely seem to find middle ground quality wise. When a worthy singer sincerely sees fit to honor in song a great influence or a departed hero, the results are often great. Way back when a young Ernest Tubb saluted Jimmy the Kid with stellar results. Merle Haggard's tribute to Bob Wills is damned good and Loretta Lynn's "I Remember Patsy" seems heartfelt and special. On the other hand, the dollar bins at used vinyl stores have been choked for years with uninspired, mediocre memorials to Hank William's often performed by third rate losers you've never heard of who of course likely never met Hank. A more modern phenomenon is the wave of compilation tribute albums that have polluted every genre of the music world. Yawn.

RCA management seems to have tried hard to come up with a worthy product here. The back cover of this album shows Buddy's parents in the studio during Skeeter's studio sessions; that's a nice touch even if they do look a bit lost in one photo. Another shows ex-Cricket and Holly family friend (and RCA artist) Waylon Jennings sitting with the Holly's, probably trying to make them feel at home.

Skeeter's voice is definitely up to the task of doing something fresh and original with Buddy's music. A double tracking technique that reminds me of that used on her hit "The End of the World" makes some of the songs sound absolutely angelic. "It Doesn't Matter Anymore" "Maybe Baby" and "True Love Ways" are all pleasantly sweet and gooey, yet just a tad bit reserved and stoic so as not to be overly maudlin.

What we have here is Skeeter singing in her familiar style. That's the way it should be. If a male voice had been picked from the RCA roster to record this album it might've degenerated into a weak and unimaginative second-rate copy of Buddy's own classic versions of his songs. Skeeter's not expected to sound like Buddy; she was free to be herself, smart move on somebody's part behind the scenes.

TAMMY WYNETTE "Greatest Hits" Epic Records. LP

Tammy's simple, dignified delivery of "Stand By Your Man" is head and shoulders above the over produced phony warbling by modern day country "divas" (I hate that overused word!). Today's spoiled little darlings sound like they've never had to mop up a toddlers puke, buy groceries on a tight budget or endure a domineering asshole husband. Tammy was real and like many great singers of humble origin her roots seem to contribute to her ability to express the lyrics of her songs. "D.I.V.O.R.C.E." could come across as mere exploitation handled by someone else; Tammy comes close to sending even me groping for my pocket hanky.

"Apartment #9" is brilliantly minimalist in arrangement keeping the spotlight wisely on Tammy's voice. How many times have we heard over the years gushing string sections over blowing songs like this? "Your Good Girls Gonna Go Bad" shows off another side of Tammy to a toe tappin' beat backed by a hot band. No doubt, much like her eventual hubby and singing partner George Jones, she was one of the absolute best country singers when it came to selling a song to us, making hum drum situations common people experience seem significant.

TANYA TUCKER "Live" MCA Records. LP.

Oh my! Look at the cover of this one. Tanya's not just hot, she's torrid, baring her navel and swinging her hips clad in a tight purple out fit. Happily, unlike many a modern day over hyped diva, she can sing as well as look sexy. This LP was recorded at the Nugget in Vegas and you can tell it wasn't no grange hall audience. You don't hear Tanya going through an “aw shucks” down home routine like she might if she was recording at the Iowa State fair. In a city where the warm-up acts are lines of long legged show girls a gal like Tanya has to flaunt her, uh... charms and her alluring voice to get over with the crowd. It’s a sign of her many years of experience that she sings to both the females in the audience with tunes like, “Would You Lay With Me (In a Field of Stone)” & “Delta Dawn” and also the men folk with rowdy numbers like “Somebody Buy This Cowgirl a Beer” and “Texas (When I Die)”.

This is a totally professional album with a well rehearsed backing band and no dead spots whatsoever. Yet even with all the glitzy Vegas trappings Tanya’s beautiful voice is intimate throughout. She seems to be singing to a handful of people in the front row You can have all those plastic, whiney, irritating broads running up and down scales like mad... I’ll take Tanya.

WANDA JACKSON “Rockin’ with Wanda” Capitol Records U.K. LP.

Yeah, yeah, yeah. I know the title of this one isn’t “square dancin’ with Wanda or “mountain cloggin’ with Wanda. Not all rockabilly albums are appropriate for inclusion in this book no matter how good they are. It all depends on how much “rock” and how much “billy” is in the grooves of the record. The icon Gene Vincent may have been a big fan of Frizell and Tubb but his ‘50’s Capitol Records output doesn't reflect it. Wanda Jackson worked on the road in the employ of none other than the great Hank Thompson at the beginning of her career. Now that's some damn fine country credentials.

Only a purist snob would whine that she's not country enough on this fine album. Included here is what just may be the ultimate country-rock and roll crossover "I Gotta Know." The song's introduction and chorus is a slow mournful fiddle lick that periodically jumps into full-blown r&r mode with hep cat lyrics. Wanda 's voice is truly amazing; she can sing just as cute and girlie as a bug's ear and next song peel the paint off the walls. If you've never heard her belt out "Fujiyama Mama" or "Let's Have a Party" you've been missing out. Wanda has reigned unchallenged as my favorite female vocalist since I first was steered to her music in the early '80's.

WENDY DAWN "Harper Valley PTA" (1969) RCA/Camden. LP.

I may be wrong, but it seems to me that somebody at RCA wanted a "girl singer" to cover the title song in a hurry in order to capitalize on its success since it was released by a small unknown label. Unfortunately, this album didn't sell enough copies to justify Wendy Dawn (if that's her real name) a gal from Memphis, Texas (according to the back cover notes) being listed in any of my record guides.

I can't even speculate on why this didn't sell. The musicians are the same topnotch ones you hear on a jillion other RCA albums. Wendy's voice is certainly up to snuff. Even though, her version of the title track isn't as full of energy as Jeannie C. Riley's, she handles "D-I-V-O-R-C-E" quite well, and her enunciation of the words in "Only Mama That'll Walk the Line," are actually a bit more understandable than Waylon's fantastic version. "Promises Promises" is a feisty Loretta Lynn type song sung damned well. When Wendy sings "House of the Rising Sun" she's good enough to make me forget she's probably the thousandth recording artist to tackle it. So, what went wrong? Did she go back to Texas and give up singing? Or is she still singing in some Amarillo honky-tonk today?

I'd like to know. I really like this album and wish she had recorded more.

5. HANKS

HANK WILLIAMS "24 Greatest Hits" (1947-1950) MGM. LP/CD

Ladies and gentlemen here's your CHAMPEEN. The undisputed PEOPLE'S champion of country music for damn sure for the last 60 years: the mighty HANK WILLIAMS SR.

Even though it's a mostly silly endeavor to rank albums (there's no proof logically one's better than the next) the superiority of this one and of Hank himself over the rest of the genre only requires a bit of jolly justification. Using pro-wrestling parlance let's examine a few other hypothetical candidates for country music's throne.

WEBB PIERCE: A solid contender with some slick holds. In a shorter 10-12 best song contest he can maybe match ol' Hank blow for blow. This 24-song album is so loaded with essential songs that are a part of the fabric of millions and millions of fans lives that it's just impossible for Webb to hang in there; you can hear him huffing and puffing in fact about song fifteen. Hank's got Webb in a headlock and he's pounding him in the face with great tunes: "Your Cheatin' Heart" "I'm so Lonesome I Could Cry" "Jambalayla" "Why Don't You Love Me" "Hey Good Lookin'" "Cold Cold Heart" and "Kawliga" on and on and on. Hell, you could probably stake another tier of twelve different songs not included on this double album up against Webb or anybody else and Hank would still carry home the strap. Let's see, we'll start with "My Son Calls Another Man Daddy" "Long Gone Lonesome Blues" and "I'll Never Get Out of this World Alive."

JIMMIE RODGERS: A sentimental favorite of many folks with good reason. Jimmie the kid certainly paved the damned way for Hank (and everybody else) as much as any singer from his time. Hank could just whomp Rodgers over the head with his huge catalog of lean, perfect songs to outlast him and retain the championship.

ROY ACUFF: A run of the mill, journeyman contender with some clear skills in his youth. I can't take his humble and sincere songs too seriously since I learned what an evil, petty, scheming man he was. He was so incredibly jealous of Jimmie Rodgers that he embarrassed Ralph Emery, Minnie

Pearl and Nashville in general on live TV by refusing to say even one nice thing about Jimmie, during an appearance meant to salute him. He was a major power broker behind the scenes in Nashville, which contaminates him in my eyes as a performer of heartfelt music. He was the equivalent of pro-wrestling bookers who always see to it that they keep the strap around their own waist in spite of how much fresh talent is on the roster. As far as I'm concerned, the ugly side of Nashville to this day can be traced back to behind the scenes creeps like him.

GARTH BROOKS? Is a Big Mac, the best tasting hamburger or rather the best seller? Mr. Brooks doesn't even crack my top 1,000,000 albums of all time; if you take issue with this critical judgment on my part I suggest you are reading the wrong damn book. Hank's immense talent choke slams Garth and his hype and boring, over produced songs for a quick 1-2-3 without breaking a sweat! WHAM!

JOHNNY CASH: A tough bout that Hank takes two out of three falls. The man in black had an amazingly long career loaded with great songs and albums. Hank was the better songwriter and of course it's obvious his example was there for Cash to follow. In the end I see these guys shaking hands and forging on together as superpower popular tag team partners as opposed to adversaries.

JOHNNY PAYCHECK: An under-rated top heel worker who can't quite get past Hank. He deserves to hold the hardcore title for sure. It's a shame most country music fans aren't even aware of his best work. I hope this book can do something to change that.

HANK WILLIAMS "Alone and Forsaken" (1995) Mercury Records. CD.

Of course, like many of my friends and I any true Hank Williams fan will break down and buy the Complete HANK WILLIAMS eight CD box set. If you don't you're missing out on a lot of great songs. Obviously most contemporary Hank Sr. CD releases contain some sort of combination of his most familiar forty or so songs. This disc is an exception to the rule of sorts. It seems to be aimed at alternative rock fans that are into melancholy music and has an introduction track by a guy from a band over in the U.K. who appears to love Hank's music but not country music in general. Well, nobody's perfect. I hope he's wised up over the years since this was released and realized that like anybody else he's only fooling himself if he's worked himself into a state of mind where he can only enjoy the music of one single country artist. At any rate, I skip over the spoken word introduction track by that dude every time I play this.

Track two "Alone and Forsaken" is a song of despair in which nature itself seems to be in a dark state of confusion. This is one of many demo recordings in which Hank is only accompanied by his guitar. "Please Don't Let Me Love You" is in my opinion, Hank's most under heard great song. He stretches out the word p-l-e-a-s-e with a pitiful sob. It's a shame that most Hank fans have probably never heard this one. "(I heard that) Lonesome Whistle" and "I'll Never Get Out of this World Alive" are usually left off of Hank re-issue CDs although they stand with his very best work.

"I've Been Down that Road Before" is a bittersweet spoken word tune that could have been inspired by one of the many beatings he took as an out of control drunk. Again it's top-notch Hank material that's rarely heard. "I Can't Escape from You" finds Hank in an absolutely hellish state of mind. Try this song with a few triple shots of Jim Beam and the lights down and you'll swear Hank is in the room with you. By God, this is why Hank Williams is the grand poobah of country music. It's just an obscure demo tune yet it's miles beyond anything ever recorded by almost any artist in this book. In the final track Hank leads us by the hand to the graveyard and sadly asks if we're prepared to meet the "Angel of Death." Whereas Jimmie Rodgers seems to look the grim reaper in the eye in the last verse of his "T.B. Blues" Hank sounds sort of unsure and uncomfortable.

Don't listen to this CD in a noisy room. Experience it alone at the end of an all night drunk for maximum effect. Unless your heart is as cold as a mackerel hot tears will scald your cheeks before it's over.

LUKE the DRIFTER JR. Volume II (1969) MGM. LP.

Hank Williams Jr. convincingly tackles some of his daddy's recitation and moralizing story songs such as "Pictures from Life's Other Side" and "Too Many Parties and Too Many Pals." Some '60's tunes that fit in are included too like "Custody" which unfortunately a lot of us can identify with. Are the songs old fashioned? Oh definitely, but is that bad? Hell, they were "old fashioned" when Hank Sr. recorded 'em, but that never stopped me, or his worldwide legion of fans from enjoying them. Hank Jr. became so famous later on in the '80's that it seems like a lot of his older albums like this have been virtually forgotten for the time being. Let's hope this book helps educate them, friends and neighbors.

Hank Williams Jr. "HANK LIVE" (1987) LP.

Sure as hell this must be the loudest damned country album of all time. This wasn't recorded in some tiny little theater, the venues were huge. The sound mix is like that of the very loudest southern rock bands and electric guitars dominate. If it weren't for Hank Jr.'s familiar voice you'd think most of side one was a loud-ass rock band like the Stones playing in a stadium. This is not a bad approach. After a great introduction by Merle Kilgore, Bocephus walks the fans through a hit parade with improvisational chatter about his daddy and his mom in between. He doesn't just run through the set, he changes words in every song. His attitude is captured in high gear. "I Really Like Girls" kicks ass; "If You Don't Like Hank Williams" has the huge crowd singing along as excited as any rock audience.

"Sweet Home Alabama" and "La Grange" are rocked out damn well to end side one. Side two finds Hank Jr. in a little bit quieter mood for awhile as he delivers acoustic partial versions of several songs any dedicated Bocephus fan knows; "The Conversation" "Man of Steel" "If Heaven ain't a lot Like Dixie" "All my Rowdy Friends," and a blistering version of a rather well known song he first recorded in the '60's "House of the Rising Sun." After a radically altered version of "The Ride" that borders on a séance, Hank wails his way through the anthem: "A Country Boy can Survive" at which point (indeed it's thee high point of the album) his loud ass band joins him and helps him close out the set. This is the ultimate album I've ever heard when it comes to this way of interpreting country music.

HANK WILLIAMS JR "Major Moves" (1984) Warner/Curb. LP.

Ol' Bocephus suddenly got red hot again in the '80's after having recorded already for a quarter century or so. By the time this LP was released he had pretty much shut up all of his father's fans that wanted him to stick to singing old school style. His success was especially impressive because he had (in the great American tradition) earned his own fortune using his own special talents as opposed to safely sticking close to his daddy's style.

The leadoff track here, "All My Rowdy Friends are Coming Over Tonight" has over the years become synonymous with Monday Night Football and therefore a treasured bauble of Americana. "Video Blues," proves once again that Hank truly understands the daily problems of "common" people. It's easy to picture him stomping around his hunting lodge drinking Jim Beam from the bottle cussing his head off while trying to hook up an '80's era VCR

. "Attitude Adjustment" is a sort of modernized take on his pappy's "I've Been Down that Road Before." Both songs have a bit of a tragic edge; both father and son have certainly had their share of domestic troubles. "Mr. Lincoln" is a social commentary number that sounds natural enough coming from Hank Jr. even though I don't think country music fans would accept it from very many other singers. So many folks perceive him as country royalty as opposed to other first generation singers and as a result he can speak his mind without fear of jeopardizing his career.

The "Blues Medley" featuring guests Ray Charles and John Lee Hooker is unexpected, well-performed and further proof of his depth as a musician. It's been obvious for many years that whereas a few thousand dumbasses who don't even like country music in the first place know him as the redneck who sings the Monday Night Football song. Hank Williams Jr. is a versatile talent whose love of music has lead him down paths most country singers don't have the interest or the freedom to travel down.

HANK WILLIAMS JR. "Rowdy" (1981) Elektra Records. LP.

Being brash, rambunctious and opinionated is Bocephus at his best. This is one of his absolute finest of many great albums. The cover sets the mood by showing him cuddling and cooing with a couple tavern cuties, all three of 'em swinging bottles and mugs. You never saw George Morgan pose on a cover like that! Side one begins with an anthem: "Dixie on My Mind" and continues with a song celebrating the obvious superiority of Texas Women. "Give a Damn" is one of many socially conscious songs that Hank has pulled off over the years. As I've pointed out elsewhere, the American country audience will accept ethical criticism from damned few singers. Johnny Cash and Hank Jr. are two who have been repeatedly tolerated for speaking their mind. "Footlights" is a revealing insiders look at Hank's duties as a professional country music singer. The very best is saved for last: Hank confronting the memory of his daddy with Waylon's "Are You Sure Hank Done it This Way?" Waylon provides the harmonizing making it an instant all time classic. Your grandma probably wouldn't like this album, but overall it's a good rowdy one to crush and blow holes in beer cans to.

HANK WILLIAMS Jr. "The Pressure is On" (1981) Elektra/Curb.

A landmark album from Bocephus' strongest period ever in his long recording career. "A Country Boy Can Survive" proves that Hank Jr. is no mere second-generation singer; he deep down understands rural people just like his daddy did. His critics, and there are swarms of 'em--don't value the potent self-sufficiency skills exhibited by what they simply consider a "buncha dumb rednecks." If these folks had their way country people would be forced to live like city people and learn to talk without southern accents and endure their city gun laws that don't make sense to folks living outside of crime ridden heavily populated areas.

I personally say fuck all that nonsense. Country people are strong and resourceful when it comes to dealing with their environment. This great anthem is no exaggeration.

"All My Rowdy Friends Have Settled Down" is a melancholy classic that gets five stars for originality in my book. I don't recall ever hearing another song quite like it. The "Ballad of Hank Williams" is a hilarious duet with Hank Sr.'s steel guitar player Don Helms. The highlight of any Hank Jr. album is the song about his daddy and Jr. really pegs him in this one. Sr. isn't revered like a saint or mourned instead the song makes fun of his frequent drunken firing of his band borrowing from the well-known Johnny Horton tune the "Battle of New Orleans." At the end of the song when the steel legend Helms points out that Bocephus fired him too once in the '70's, Jr. deadpans: "well... it's a family tradition!" YUK YUK.

HANK WILLIAMS III "Lovesick Broke & Driftin'" (2002) Curb Records. CD.

I love the hell out of most of HANK III's first CD "Risin' Outlaw" but after reading him bash it to a couple interviewers, I've decided to forego including it. This disc though is as essential as the bottle of Beam behind the bar at yer local watering hole. HANK III hasn't just eased his way into the world of country music; he's come roaring in like a gaggle of drunk and pissed party crashers on Harley's.

From what I've observed music journalists seem to all compete with one another to portray Hank III as an almost eerie reincarnation of his grandfather. I'm the first to agree that he does Hank Sr.'s sort of music justice. "One Horse Town" features some fine down and out Hank Senior-ish lyrics and some lovely damn yodeling. "Walking with Sorrow" flat out gives me goose bumps. I heard him sing it live before this CD was released and although I had heard it just once, it stuck in my head permanently. For some damned reason I began to think of Hank III and that song every time I heard a little birdie whistling in a tree. I thought about that, and figured maybe he had whistled during his live version of the song. Hell, I don't know. Suffice it to say the song played over and over in my head on many occasions after only one listening, which becomes a really remarkable factoid when you consider how drunk I was at the show.

Well, back to the album at hand. Yes, HANK III does know how to deliver a song like his grandpa when it suits him. Likewise he sounded occasionally at this stage of his career a bit like his old man too. An awful lot of the same "music journalists" who express their love for Hank Sr. seem to bend over backwards to either ignore Hank Jr. and his genetic influence on HANK III, or to directly slag him by referring to him smugly as "that Monday Night Football guy." These dumb asses really don't know what the hell they're talking about. Regardless of the relationship between father and son (remember folks... we can only speculate... as Hank Sr. would say: "mind your own business") HANK III's music owes a bit to his dad and his grandpa's. The family attitude has been handed down as well. "Trashville," is as sure to piss off as many industry people in Nashville as Hank Jr.'s rebellion against the suits did many years ago.

BUT! Occasional family influence aside, HANK III is his own man and has his own sound and his own way of doing things just like his forebears. That's what makes him really great. He ordinarily plays two or more sets on a given night a "country" set followed (after a series of warnings to the audience) by a loud and rocking set that makes him one of the most innovative acts going. His brand of metal is actually incredibly creative, including a fiddle and electric standup bass. When I saw it all live I detected a faint country edge during some of the metal songs. Like I said, HANK III is his own man and an innovator not content to rest on the family laurels.

III is obviously an imbiber who loves to get messed up. "Mississippi Mud" is a joyous celebration of that. Drinking oriented songs like "…Mud" along with "Whiskey Weed and Women" and "5 shots of whiskey" earn extra points for HANK III in a day and age in which boring and sappy relationship songs dominate country radio.

In a perfect world Hank III would gallop to the top of the country charts with his country songs and to the top of the pop charts with his metal numbers. I'm not holding my breath, but it's gonna be hard for the biz creeps to sweep him under the rug when he's got so much talent.

HANK SNOW "The Best of" (1966) RCA. LP.

Between his recording career that began in Canada in 1936 and his death in 1999, "Hank" Clarence E. Snow sandwiched in more "Best of" and "Greatest Hits" albums than most artists first time around releases. It's almost mind boggling to realize that there's a banner headline on the back cover liner notes to this LP that read: "A Great Veteran's Greatest."

Damn. He was still in his prime. Well, RCA had plenty of old tracks to choose from including a handful of the greatest country songs ever recorded such as "The Golden Rocket" "I'm Movin' on" and "I've been everywhere." Mr. Snow was never one to record smutty tunes or songs celebrating drinking alcohol; that would seriously hamper quite a few singers to be sure. To compensate, he seemed to make his songs interesting by staying a step ahead of the honky tonk singers when it came to inventive rhythms and catchy melodies.

His voice was different from the rest of the Opry pack too owing to his Canadian roots. He sounded like no one else that came before him. Of course nowadays Nashville would shake its monstrous head and point to the door if Hank Snow came around auditioning. Even Moe Bandy and Joe Stampley were sex pots compared to the plain looking "Singing Ranger." If he and Red Sovine went out trolling for chicks it's hard to say who'd get first pick. It's a good thing he came along when he did.

HANK SNOW "I've Been Everywhere" (1963) RCA. LP.

Songs about romance and adventure in far away places enjoyed a great deal of popularity throughout a lot of the twentieth century. Unfortunately, in this day and age foreign name place songs don't exactly summon up mental images of exotic beaches and love at first sight. The first things that typically come to mind when you mention overseas travel are terrorists, diarrhea, bombs and socially transmitted diseases.

The good old days are fun to look back upon though. You can get lost in this batch of globetrotting Snow tunes. The lead off song is the jolly tongue twister "I've Been Everywhere." He goes on to visit Japan ("Geisha Girl") Australia (Melba from Melbourne") Alaska ("Springtime in Alaska") before landing back home ("In the Blue Canadian Rockies"). No wild experiments here or breaks from the tried and true tasteful Snow style of arrangement, one of many thoughtful, professional and irresistible, Snow albums.

HANK THOMPSON "A Six Pack to Go" ('60's re-issue) LP.

I'll tell you why Hank Thompson was so great; he specialized in the two things you still have to do to excel as a honky tonk singer and bandleader in Texas. You've got to sell a lot of damn beer and you've got to keep the folks on the dance floor happy. It all works hand in hand; hot sweaty dancers drink a helluva lot more beer than wallflowers. This collection of drinking oriented Thompson tunes is almost impossible to top. Enthusiastic drinking anthems like "Six Pack to Go" and it's followed up with "Hangover Tavern" to get you up on your feet swilling brews, loosening up your inhibitions.

Next you grab you a gal and dance to the "Bartenders Polka." Hank recorded entire albums of instrumental dance tunes. You're in good hands here. As the evening goes by Hank slows it down once in a while with a tearjerker for the lovelorn lined up at the bar such as his immortal cheater anthem, "Wild Side of Life" included here. In Texas dance halls this sort of song always leads to a run on the bar for entirely different reasons than cooling off from dancing. You think of that two timing witch who dumped you and need to get shit faced. Bandleader Thompson was a master of squeezing in songs for every kind of drunk in the tavern from the happy guys blowing their paycheck to the somber losers at love. This album is as consistently good as a 12-pack of sparkling icy cold Lone Star long necks.

HANK THOMPSON "North of the Rio Grande" (1955) Capitol. LP.

Whereas some of the great Mr. Thompson's albums over the years concentrated on a dance or western theme this particular album showcases Mr. Thompson's versatile mastery of multiple country styles popular in the 1950's.

"Big Beaver" and "Panhandle Rag" are two topnotch dance numbers that Hank and his Brazos Valley Boys undoubtedly regularly unleashed in Texas saloons way back when. “Dusty Skies” is a western cattle drive ballad. “Baby I Need Lovin’” is an example of perfect pleasant honky tonk pop while “Where My Sweet Baby Used to Walk” and “I’d do it Again” are introspective and a tad bit philosophical. “The Little Rosewood Casket” will have you reaching for a hankie and a double shot to go with yer Lone Star. All in all there’s not a bad or dull tune on this album. As usual the band is first rate. You simply can’t go wrong with Hank Thompson albums from this decade or the one following it.

HANK THOMPSON “State Fair of Texas” (early ‘60’s) Capitol. LP.

A great batch of songs, but in spite of the picture of fifty-two foot “Big Tex” on the cover and all the various sonic efforts included to convince you otherwise, this album wasn’t recorded at no damned state fair. The 1960’s era was chockablock with phony “live” albums from several other music genres for that matter so lets judge Hank by the music and not the transparent gimmick.

Side one starts with “Deep in the Heart of Texas” long one of our state’s most important anthems. “My Heart is a Playground” is loaded with fair buzzwords and was probably written in Hank’s shower in ten minutes, but what the hell, it’s a perfect festive number for the occasion. “Rub-a-dub-dub” is a crowd pleaser (even though the crowd is likely a couple studio engineers). Side two is super strong with two more Texas songs ”Beautiful Texas” and my favorite “There’s a Little Bit of Everything in Texas.”

I almost forgot to mention the sounds of the midway, sideshows and several minutes of the Texas/Oklahoma annual football game included. Yeah, by today's sophisticated standards this album’s as carney as the “volcano” at a goofy-golf course, but the bottom line truth is it brings a smile to my lips and makes me want to plan a trip to Dallas for the State fair.

HANK THOMPSON “Smoky the Bar” Dot Records. LP.

In the late 1960’s and early ‘70’s a helluva lot of country musicians tried to make their music seem up to date to the hippie pop culture audience by various means. The Stonemans posed wearing hippie clothing on an album cover that seems shameful today in a way, but even many of the biggest stars were growing their hair out and using psychedelic graphic layouts to try to seem “with it.” Not so Hank Thompson, who never seemed to waver. The back cover liner notes declare him the “poet laureate of beer drinkers” and I’ll drink to that!

The title song “Smoky the Bar” is a sort of philosophical reassertion of the sacredness of one of our nations finest institutions: the great American honky tonk. “Ace in the Hole” follows, but the words are different from the various other versions I’ve heard sung by folks ranging from Irish folk singers to softer spoken less opinionated country singers than Hank. It targets non-self sufficient hippies of the day out protesting various causes and their apparent knack for getting others to support them.

Hank doesn't linger on current events long, he merely draws a sort of line in the spit riddled sawdust on the bar room floor. Next up is the great "Let's get Drunk and be Somebody" which I agree is a great antidote for whatever ails you. "Cocaine Blues" is delivered in a rowdy manor that shows that Hank T. is at his most aggressive on this album. The intensity of "Drunkards Blues" and "What's made Milwaukee Famous" left me staring at my glass trying to summon the strength to fetch another round from my cooler. A version of "Pop a Top" picks me up and ends the album with an upbeat anthem. A well-chosen batch of songs that all run together perfectly.

6. HONKY TONK

CHARLIE WALKER "Greatest Hits" Columbia Records. LP.

Just as much as Hank or Ernest or Faron the lesser-known Charlie Walker was born to sing in honky tonks to inebriated blue collar people. What's more, just like the big name singers Walker didn't need any gimmicks or novelty voices or production to get his songs over with the people. That's what real country music has always been about, picking your guitar or sawing away at your fiddle while singing simple words that apply loosely to the lives of working people. Some of Walker's songs were tailored to appeal to cocky and confident beer drinkers and hell raisers such as “Pick Me Up On Your Way Down” and “Who Will Buy the Wine.”

Other songs sound a bit desperate such as the apologetic; “I Don’t Mind Saying” and the conciliatory, “I’ll Catch You When You Fall.” Hey, if you’re gonna make a career singing in honky tonks you’ve got to appeal to both the drunks whose love lives are looking promising and those whose world’s are falling apart. Charlie Walker was an all-purpose honky tonk singer of the first damn rank. His voice reminds me a bit of Ernest Tubb, but he was his own man with his own hits. In other words if Tubb were a chicken fried steak platter down at Cracker Barrel, Charlie Walker would be the meat loaf plate. They each have their distinctive charms, yet most people who like one will enjoy the other.

I have no idea why he seems to have been forgotten these days compared to some other singers from his heyday. What the hell, Miller Light outsells Lone Star even in top-40 jock country hangouts and we all know which of the two is clearly better.

Ernest Tubb “Favorites” (1951) Decca Records. LP.

Over fifty years ago this was first released and these songs still are packaged and repackaged by various labels the world over. Now that’s something to hoist a cold can of Pearl to. These songs are not only immortal; many have a historic significance too on more than one level. Songs like: “Soldier’s Last Letter” “Filipino Baby” and “Seaman’s

Blues" are not only vintage topnotch quality country music, they express common sentiments of a large segment of G.I's from the post war (WWII) era. Of course "Walking the Floor Over You" is an eternal sort of ditty even the ancient Roman's or Greek's would've dug. Ditto for "Try Me One More Time" and "Sipping Around." Let's not forget the significance from an egghead's standpoint of the pioneering snappy electric lead guitar lines found in many of these songs. As much as Ernest worshipped the late great Jimmie Rodgers as a young man, he didn't merely ape him and stop there. He helped shape the modern way music of more than one genre was to be played in the 1950's.

ERNEST TUBB "Record Shop" (1960) Decca. LP.

The album cover is loaded with pictures and plugs for Ernest's Nashville record store which is dubbed in all seriousness: "The Country and Western Music Center of the World." Accompanying the hype is a dozen songs which prove that Tubb's voice is still hanging in there quite nicely at the dawn of the Space Age. It's fun to hear "He'll Have to Go" warbled through ol' Ernest's trademark gargle throat as opposed to Jim Reeves crooned version. Lots of other strong classic tunes are included such as "Who Will Buy the Wine" "Pick Me Up on Your Way Down" and "Why I'm Walkin'."

Tubb always seems to include a ballad or two meant to be especially meaningful for his legions of WWII vet fans.

This time around we have "A Guy Named Joe" penned by Harlan Howard.

All in all, a damned fine album, from stem to stern, regardless of all the publicity for his record shop. Modern day fans would probably be appalled at such blatant commercialism, but frankly, with talent like Ernest Tubb's I wouldn't care if he strolled the stage wearing a sandwich board plugging his store.

ERNEST TUBB "Saturday Satan Sunday Saint" (1968) Decca. LP.

This album was recorded during troubled times for many honky tonk icons, the heart of the hippie era. The ol' pro delivers a fine album that shows he's flexible towards modern song ideas even if his music hasn't changed much. His voice has the same familiar quaver and he still calls out the names of the boys in his band before they solo.

Several songs could have only been recorded in the late 1960's. The title track for instance, is a sort of post-Harper Valley hypocrisy number about folks who sin all week yet sit up front at church acting holy in spite of it. Joe South's pop hit, "Games People Play" is covered, but hell; it sounds like a real country song. I bet Ernest could've sung a Steppenwolf number and make it sound like his own. His voice simply takes over. "Tommy's Doll" is an incredibly progressive song about a little boy who prefers to play with a doll instead of the toy soldiers and gun his father force him to play with WHOO-EEEEE.

Not all the songs are '60's-ish. The lead off tune "She's Lookin' Better by the Minute" is an eternal gal hungry honky tonk classic. "Just a Drink Away" is a sad tale of woe about the miseries of having a gal with round heels which is firmly rooted in the past. Ernest may have changed a tad bit with the times but he never came close to singing songs you'd have been likely to hear at a love-in or an acid party. For the record, I'm happy to see he's not sporting love beads and a Nehru jacket on the cover.

FARON YOUNG "Aims at the West" (1963) Mercury Records LP

A great concept album, to showcase Faron's mighty voice, I've got to admit up front here that I'm a real sucker for TV Western theme songs. He sings the "Bonanza" theme (did you know it has words?) the "Ballad of Paladin" "Rawhide" and "The Rebel Johnny Yuma." Faron's version of the theme from the classic film "High Noon" is extremely rousing. The arrangements backing the songs are impressive being rich with twangy guitar and nice percussion effects. I'm not sure if this record was influenced by Johnny Cash's recordings of several of these titles or if Cash's label decided to capitalize on this platter. I don't really care; labels have always been quick to ape the success of a competitor. Faron and Johnny's Western songs would sound great back to back on the same cassette driving through West Texas or Wyoming.

FARON YOUNG "Sings" Faron Young Records. LP.

I love this record. I especially dig the picture of Faron on the cover wearing a loud jacket/tie/shirt combo and a shit-eating grin. I'm even partial to the label art, which is a trademark silver star over a red label. I'm impressed with the fact that Faron's own company clearly as a result of being dumped by a label pressed this album. I bet he sold these at gigs and signed them for his fans personally.

I have no idea when the songs included were recorded, perhaps some time in the 1970's. "Wine Me Up" is just a hands down, all time honky tonk great of course. "What's He Doing in My World" and "(I guess) I Had Too Much to Dream Last Night" are both intense, emotional songs. Faron was born to hard sell songs like these without ever seeming sappy. My favorite is a caustic tune "Country Girl" which is just bitter enough to bring to mind Johnny Paycheck's bitter "Lil' Darlin'," label tunes.

Faron Young was no damned crossover pop singer. Likewise, if you're looking for rockabilly or peppy blue grass arrangements don't bother with this. It's riveting country music with songs based on real life emotions, which are often ugly. Newbie fans that already discovered George Jones should gravitate to Faron Young when they're ready.

FARON YOUNG "This Little Girl of Mine" (1972) Mercury Records. LP.

This album starts out innocently enough with a heartfelt ballad for Faron's daughter "This Little Girl of Mine." Faron's shown on the back cover holding his 40th birthday cake with her (did you know he shares February 25th with my wife and legendary wrestler Ric Flair?). How nice. After the cake has been cut and the wholesome title track has been sung, the album proceeds as if he ducked out of the party early so he could meet an older gal with curves at some no-tell motel in the sleazy part of town.

The rest of the selections are very adult in the cheating sense featuring lyrics with cleverly written subtle (and in some cases not so subtle) meanings. "Forever was the Name of our Sunshine" and "One of My Sad days" look back briefly at simpler times. "Left to Right or Right to Wrong" finds him sitting on the fence deliberating his actions. He jumps into a steamy relationship with both feet in, "It Hurts so Good" "Play Now Pay Later" and especially the steamy, "A Woman's Touch."

Mr. Young was one of a handful of singers born to handle the slight nuances of the lyrics of these songs. The usual session guys plus five fiddlers sawing away as if to abstractly suggest: "You'll go to hell for this" back him. This is a top-notch album worth seeking out at all costs.

JOHNNY BOND "Ten Little Bottles" (1965) Starday. LP.

The versatile Mr. Bond's musical talents were many. He was certainly one of the top handfuls of greats of the truck driving song genre and he was no slouch when it came to western songs either. He held the championship strap though (at least amongst artists on labels the size of Starday or larger) when it came to drunken country humor. This album is obsessed with booze and that's a good thing for lots of us. I frankly was disgusted when I learned Otis the town drunk from Mayberry was in real life a sober churchgoer. There's enough straight shooters over the years who steered clear of drinking songs, it's only right that we drinkers have a few unabashed albums to savor about the joys of the jug.

There are two versions of the smash hit: "Ten Little Bottles" a single version and the complete story. One of my favorite drinking sagas "Three Sheets in the Wind" has been included thoughtfully. "Judge Roy Bean's Court" is a wacky story utilizing some familiar Hollywood voices. "Winter Blizzard" combines Mr. Bond's knack for drinking stories with his Western shtick. Hey, as I write this I'm drinking a Busch beer and sheeit… on the cover Johnny's pulling a Busch draft... WOW.

JOHNNY BUSH "Texas Dance Hall Girl" (1973) RCA. LP.

YEE HAWW! Six out of ten songs on this masterpiece are drinking songs. These songs are Texan through and through. By the way, If you've never been to the Lone Star state on a hot summer night and sucked up a bellyful of beer in an ancient honky tonk, while people from age 18 to 80 are dancing like crazy to a fiddle led band, you've never really experienced the best remaining pocket of real country music. Just like burgers in Texas are served a bit differently than smaller, less important states (with pickles and mustard) even today Texas honky tonks still operate in a different manner than in places like Nashville or Bakersfield. Come down here and visit Gruene hall in New Braunfels or Floore's country store in Helotes and you'll see what I mean.

Anyway, Mr. Bush kicks this one off with, "Dance Hall Girl," which glorifies those lovely gals he clearly loved the most from his audience. The late great Texas King of Western Swing, Bob Wills, is saluted with a cover of, "My Shoes Keep Walking Back to You." Then, Johnny slows it down and sings a loving tribute ballad to the bottle "(Wine Friend of Mine) Stand by Me" then follows up with the equally soused, "Muscatel Memories." Side two features three more wine songs back to back to back: "The Warm Red Wine" "The Genuine Healer of Time" and the album ending, "Waltz of the Wine". Bush wails from the depths of his soul on this album. WARNING! This one'll possibly send you down to the liquor store for a jug of Night Train or Thunderbird to enjoy with any subsequent listenings.

JOHNNY BUSH "Whiskey River/There Stands the Glass" (1973) RCA.

Mr. Bush poses on the cover of this one eyes closed, leaning on a bar with a half-gallon of Jack Daniels at his elbow. His fist is wrapped around a sizable glass of whiskey that would stagger a big drinker for more than a few minutes. Uuum. Just looking at it makes me thirsty. This isn't an album of happy drinking songs.

The mood is bittersweet with an emphasis on reflection and soul searching. Side one starts off with the Webb Pierce classic: "There Stands the Glass." Johnny doesn't just croon or warble, he leans back and belts it out from his gut with a heavy, heavy vibrato. It gives me goose bumps. He follows it with a Harlan Howard number appropriate to the mood he's set "Another Bridge to Burn." The end of the side is Mr. Bush's version of "Whiskey River" which is a true showstopper. All throughout this batch of songs his voice is intense. It's so impressive you may want to yank the needle up and play several songs again before going on. Side two is less boozy and the songs are a bit more conciliatory such as "Right Back In Your Arms Again" and "It's the Last Time I'll Ever Cheat On You." This album ranks Texas Johnny Bush way beyond journeymen honky tonk professionals. He's a singer's singer.

LEFTY FRIZZELL "Look What Thoughts Will Do" (1997) Columbia. Two CD set.

Lefty hit the charts in 1950 with a bang. Soon his fame and chart success rivaled that of even the great one--Hank Sr.

The two of them had a lot in common from a personal standpoint. Like Hank, by all accounts Lefty was a genuinely nice guy whose career was hampered by an awful marriage. Both of them wrote many of their songs about their wives. Hank even felt so bad about his pal Lefty's problems with Mrs. Frizzell that he wrote one about them "I'm Sorry For You My Friend."

The two were also very different in many ways. Hank was a notorious bad drunk whereas lots of Lefty's friends recall him as being a happy one. A year or so before Hank's death he and Audrey split and he remarried. Lefty unfortunately stayed with his ball and chain for a long time trying to work things out. Legend has it he wound up as a result being punished and reprimanded to the point of living in exile in the basement of his own house eating canned food heated on a hot plate. His career suffered big time as a result. It's hard to think of another country music star of his stature that faded into oblivion as sadly as he did.

Hank's legend has endured over the years. Lefty these days are almost unknown to the masses, yet he lives on through the voices of others. Whereas virtually every Opry star of note these days has been instructed by their publicists to praise Hank the guy who is stylistically emulated most often by the same batch of singers is Lefty. His vocal phrasing is (pardon the expression) "modern". Veteran artists Merle Haggard and Randy Travis both owe a helluva lot to Lefty Frizzell as well. Merle has recorded an album of his songs to pay tribute and Travis has always been forthcoming about his influences and has sung a lot of great songs that plainly reflect Lefty's influence on him.

Give Mr. Frizzell a listen and I'm sure you'll agree that his vocals are amazingly contemporary in an almost eerie way. His last hit from 1963, "Saginaw Michigan" sounds a damn site more recent than 40 years old.

Let's not hold that against him though. Real live fiddlers, guitarists and piano players as opposed to being whipped up by synth and sample happy producers backed his songs. He left behind a legacy of honky tonkin' anthems my favorites being: "If You've Got the Money I've Got the Time" "Shine Shave Shower (It's Saturday)" and "I'm An Old Old Man (Tryin' to Live While I Can)." His song of contrition to his domineering spouse, "I Love You a Thousand Ways" is an all-time classic of its type even if it does make me feel sorry for his squandered sincerity. His take on Jimmie the kid's, "My Rough and Rowdy Ways" is as praiseworthy as anybody else's from over the years. Several of his songs are so infectious I just sit in front of the CD player with a bottle in one hand pushing the little reverse arrow button with the other: "You're Humbuggin' Me" "Don't Think it Ain't Been Fun Dear (Cuz it Ain't)" and the maudlin but timeless, "Mom and Dad's Waltz."

There are reissue LPs to be found with ten or so Lefty songs, but I'd hold out for this anthology or something similar. His very best days preceded the album era and like other guys who go that far back you may as well bite the bullet and have a CD collection you'll treasure forever.

RAY PRICE "Greatest Hits" Columbia Records. LP.

As you might expect, there's been a helluva lot of Ray Price hits collections released over the years. This one stands even taller than the rest. It's loaded with many of his earliest blue ribbon winners that are so uniquely good they can be played back to back with Hank Sr. And Ernest Tubb's best of the '50's and measure up damn well. Now I know that later in life Mr. Price recorded a lot of softer music backed by cliché strings, but back in the day his records were pure, genuine honky tonk.

"Crazy Arms" for instance, just oozes the ambiance of a 1950's saloon. It's definitely one of the most perfect country music songs ever recorded from the lyrics and chord progression to the power and emotion in Ray's voice and the beautiful, perfectly balanced backing vocal. It's no coincidence these tunes are so great when you consider that Ray studied at the feet of Hank Williams himself in his final days. He roomed with him even and tried to steer him away from trouble to the extent that anybody could.

He even substituted for him at shows when Hank was too annihilated to perform. What better way to learn the ropes? Ray proved he learned quite a bit from Hank by going on to record a string of deliciously raw, lovesick classics including "Heartaches By the Number" and "Release Me." Not only that, Ray's rich rendition of the Bob Wills classic: "My Shoes Keep Walking Back to You" is the best of the dozen or so versions I've heard. This album is not only loaded, it sounds even better when I'm loaded. I can entertain myself with this small batch of songs for hours.

TEX RITTER "Blood on the Saddle" (1960) Capitol Records. LP.

We are informed by the liner notes on the back of this album that Mr. Ritter started out as a singing lecturer billed as "The Texas Cowboy and His Songs." I wish I had been around to witness one of his spiels. I'm a longtime Louis L'Amour and Elmer Kelton fanatic and it seems to me that Tex Ritter's music is a sort of musical equivalent. He doesn't just croon the words to the songs; he lives out their various moods like an actor might.

"When the Work's All Done This Fall" and "The Face on the Bar Room Floor" are fine narrative story songs you can hunker down in your chair and focus on. Tex sounds absolutely soused on the albums best song: "Rye Whiskey" which is a great tune to knock back a shot or two (or three... or four...) to. "Blood On the Saddle" and "Bury Me Not On the Lone Prairie" are shot knockers too although they are grim and serious.

By the end of the album, I've downed enough shots of Rye that I'm no longer angry that the lyrics to the "Billy the Kid" song seem to be based on lies perpetuated for too many years. Don't blame Tex for that, just pass the bottle and flip the LP over again.

WEBB PIERCE "Hayride Boogie 1950-1951" Krazy Kat Records. LP

These songs were recorded during Hank Williams Sr.'s. peak years. No one knew he'd be gone so soon, but waiting in the wings to take over was Webb Pierce. This album is a great collection of extremely obscure Pierce recordings he sold early in his careers to tiny record labels. At this point in time he was like an AAA level pitcher clocking 100 mph fastballs.

His delivery was totally there even if the fans and the journalists didn't know it yet. Lefty Frizzell was great, but Webb's, "California Blues" "In the Jailhouse Now" and "Freight Train Blues" remove all doubt that he was the top prospect of his generation at interpreting Jimmie Rodgers style. "I Need You Like a Hole in the Head" is a Hank style song in which Webb delivers the goods especially well. "Hayride Boogie" is the initial version of a number that eventually evolved into the rockabilly anthem "Teenage Boogie" several years later. The sound quality of this collection is superb making it essential to dig up some how considering I doubt that many were pressed.

WEBB PIERCE "Memory #1" (mid '60's) Decca. LP

So many Pierce albums were released over the years that featured re-recordings, it can be confusing to know what versions of his songs you're getting when you buy one. The fact is some are definitely more worth having than others. This album's got several great tunes and a couple I'm not in a hurry to listen to again. Two of the best are originals: "As

Long As I'll Forgive" and "Waiting a Lifetime" both of which have that magic of vintage Webb material.

If you're as obsessed with drinking songs, as I am you just can't help but enjoy "Here I am Drunk Again" and "I'm Gonna Hang One on Tonight." That's Where My Money Goes" and "Memory #1". Both tickle my fancy big time. The less I say about "French Riviera" (which sounds like it could've been rejected from one of the more forgettable Elvis Presley movie soundtracks) the better. I like the lengthy back cover liner notes by Webb's "secretary." Today's overly slick pop-country releases could use a homey bit of hokum like that.

WEBB PIERCE "Webb with a Beat" (1960) Decca. LP.

To be honest I've always tapped my toe to the beat in Webb's earlier material. I guess the title is meant to refer to the prominent snare played on the offbeat and boosted up fairly high in the mix. This album was recorded at a time of course when rock and roll was threatening to put country music out of business. The extremely odd liner notes on the back of this album are loaded with industry jargon that blatantly points out that other artists are trying to cleverly "cash in" on a modernized pop beat, shamelessly explaining in the process that this album features the "new sound of Webb Pierce."

I don't think the beat is that much higher octane. "I Ain't Never" is a toe-tapper but it's nowhere close to sounding like rock and roll or rockabilly. "Gotta Travel On" is full of pep, but again it sounds like good old Webb not a new and improved incarnation. When he slows things down for "Poison Love" "I'm Tired" and "Is it Wrong (for loving you)" he sounds completely at home. I can't say the same for the one big clinker on this album "I've Got My Fingers Crossed" which is a blatant rip off of the pop hit "Special Angel" with teen heartthrob trappings.

The album is closed out well with Webb's classic cover of Jimmie Rodgers: "In the Jailhouse Now," which blots the dumbass liner notes out of my mind.

7. NASHVILLE-THE GOOD YEARS

"3 COUNTRY GENTLEMEN" Locklin/Snow/Wagoner (1963)RCA. LP.

This is the country offering from a popular 1960's RCA album series each of which featured three great talents from a selected genre. Hank Locklin starts things off with a slow and intense version of a familiar favorite about love gone down the toilet: "Ivory Tower." Hank Snow is represented well with the western ballad, "Laredo" and a bizarre tale of a soldier being rescued by a native fellow with a bone through his nose titled "Black Diamond." Porter Wagoner seizes the limelight though with a pretty but sad number, "False True Lover" followed by an even prettier and sadder number in which the animal kingdom becomes unhinged over a broken down romance "They Listened While You Said Goodbye."

He closes out the album with the bittersweet "Eat Drink and Be Merry (For Tomorrow You'll Cry").

Being a devoted disciple of all three of these kingpins of country music, I certainly don't want to run them down needlessly. I simply can't avoid though pointing out the unusually ugly photos on the cover. They all look like "before" pictures for a big ear syndrome remedy. Zits, false teeth, 5 O'clock shadows... yuck! These must be amongst the worst pictures of these guys ever. It's as if the photo collage were assembled by a jealous RCA colleague who didn't pass muster for this "3 of a kind" series album. HHmmm, perhaps Eddy Arnold?

BILLY STRANGE "Great Western Themes" (1960's) GNP Records. LP

TV Westerns and twangy guitars go together like hardtack and beans; like rye whiskey and hand rolled smokes; like trail dust and the scent of cowshit. I don't care if you're from the USA or Italy or New Zealand. Most of you who lived through the 1960's and '70's would think immediately of Western TV shows and movies if you heard this album of instrumentals. I'm well aware that heavily reverb tinged guitars are hardly authentic from a historical standpoint. So what? When I hear Billy Strange's version of "The Magnificent Seven" I am reminded of things Western just as much as when I hear a Tex Ritter platter. "The Good the Bad and the Ugly" is synonymous with the old American West around the globe to folks who don't speak English and haven't been within several time zones of Texas. Billy Strange's ominous twanging on this album is similar to guitar sounds that began to be heard in the 1960's on albums by country honcho's like Johnny Cash and Merle Haggard to name just two. He runs through the themes from TV's "Bonanza" "Gunsmoke" and "Have Gun Will Travel" here as well as a handful of originals. Take my word for it; this is perfect music to listen to while passing a whiskey bottle around a campfire.

BOBBY BARE "Bare" (1978) Columbia Records. LP.

The late '70's through the early '80's was a great period for Bobby Bare. All of his albums from this stretch are noteworthy for the caliber of songs he recorded. Of course some of them (including this one) were packed with Shel Silverstein songs, which pretty much guarantees an eclectic batch of quality numbers. For example on side one he contributed "Yard Full of Rusty Cars" which describes spending a night in a tiny trailer out in the middle of nowhere with a family similar to the one described in David Allan Coe's "If That Aint Country." Immediately following it is "Greasy Grit Gravy" which is a hilarious take on all the goofy foods discriminating country folk consider delicacies.

Silverstein didn't however pen the equally amusing "Big Dupree" (which concludes with a falsetto verse due to the nature of the injury sustained by the narrator of the song) and "Finger On the Button" which manage to express some sympathy in a good-natured way for the President of the US without being partisan in any way.

Side two is loaded with a batch of Silverstein creations that are more serious and almost high brow in nature including the excellent "This Guitar is for Sale" and "Childhood Hero" which are both a bit introspective without ever sounding sappy or embarrassing. This is probably as solid as any country album recorded in 1978 even though Bobby Bare wasn't as high profile as some other country music legends were at the time.

BOBBY BARE "The Best of" (1966) RCA. LP.

In retrospect, it was rather early in his career for a greatest hits LP, but who can tell if a singer will keep going after a few successful albums or fade away? If you could tell which singers are gonna prevail and become superstars your services would be in demand by record labels worldwide. You can't though… so forget I brought it up.

Bobby's first "musical milestone" (recorded under a pseudonym) is included in this album. It's a song titled: "All-American Boy" which is a light-hearted look at the rags to riches success (and then on into the US army) of guys like Elvis. Ironically, it's said that Bobby couldn't capitalize on the success of the single at the time because Uncle Sam drafted his ass.

Some of these hits are rather weighty such as: "Detroit City" "Times Are Gettin' Hard" and "500 Hundred Miles" but Bobby never irritates me like many of the whiny, dour faced folkies of the early '60's do. Even though this album pre-dates his work with legendary writer Shel Silverstein, Mr. Bare already had found an effective voice for delivering ironic lyrics "Dear Wastebasket" is a fine example.

"Millers Cave" and "I'd Fight the World" are both topnotch numbers worthy of mention. A damned strong album, although the typical '60's background choral arrangements will bother some hardcore purists.

BOBBY BARE "Drunk and Crazy" (1980) CBS Records. LP.

A truly stupendous album that's chockablock with so many creative songs, it's the high water mark of the Silverstein-Bare tag team. This album is so great, It should be studied by contemporary Nashville artists, producers and writers as a blueprint for how to get un-real country music back on track after years of cranking out boring albums filled often with the same old relationship songs.

The title track "Drunk and Crazy," is both danceable and fun for sodden wallflowers like me to listen to. It's a rowdy anthem that serves notice this isn't going to be a batch of solemn, introspective crap. Track two is "The World's Last Truck Driving Man" a mindblowing sci-fi tune that breathes new life into the trucking sub-genre. "Food Blues" flips the bird at pompous nutrition nuts. Highlights of side two include "Your Credit Card Won't Get You into Heaven" "Tequila Sheila" and another anthem: "Drinkin' and Druggin' and Watchin' TV."

This album is incredibly under rated. Virtually every review I can find of it on the Internet is favorable yet oblivious to the truth that it goes on beyond the usual high standard of Bare albums. For years I've been telling my personal friends to get this at all costs. You don't even need to be a country fan to appreciate songs this good. Do you have ears? What more can I say?

BOBBY BARE "Hard Time Hungry's" (1975) RCA LP

Bobby and tune smith Shel Silverstein go together about as well as "Paycheck and Mayhew," "Jones and Wynette." Hell, even "Moe and Joe," the back of the album sleeve art tells the story. A grungy looking guy in an overcoat is hunched over a garbage can in an alley, eating his breakfast. In the upper left hand corner of the sleeve it reads: "A Concept by Shel Silverstein."

It becomes plain soon that this isn't Porter Wagoner's boozehound alter ego "Skid-Row Joe" in the alley. He ain't drunk, he's not lovelorn, he's hungry damnit.. The title song "Hardtime Hungry's," leads off side one and sets the stage for an album of songs examining poverty, joblessness and in general being economically challenged. Between the songs is woven a series of dialogues with plain folk talking about their own hard times. This is a nice touch even though the sound quality makes it occasionally hard to understand what the folks are saying.

"Alimony" and "$100,000 in Pennies" are perfectly biting Silverstein style ditties. "Daddy's Been Around the House Too Long" is an effective number seen as from a child's innocent point of view. "Back Home in Huntsville Again" takes matters to another unique extreme. Mr. Bare's delivery of Shel's words is as usual fantastic. I find myself getting up and swinging the tone arm of my turntable back to play certain lines dead panned or slurred or otherwise given the Bare treatment. He's that good. He's not just a pretty voice in a genre saturated with them. He makes you focus on the words in the same way Johnny Cash (another veteran crooner of Silverstein songs) did.

Incidentally, the songs in this album are not preachy or politically slanted unlike a lot of folk music I've heard covering the "issue" of hunger. Bobby simply paints a series of realistic pictures with the words and then sort of backs on out for the listener to think on.

BOBBY BARE "The Streets of Baltimore" (1966) RCA LP

This is a "concept" album every bit as much as Bobby's label-mate Porter's albums from this period are. The songs are mostly melancholy expressions of the city not being as great as it seemed from afar. Bare's big hit song: "The Streets of Baltimore" provides a nice theme to build an album around. Dean Martin's hit "Houston" fits the mold well as does "Early Morning Rain" and "Changin' My Mind."

"There Ain't No Fun in This Town" drives the point home and the album ends with Bobby's rendition of the tragic epic "Green Green Grass of Home" as if to remind us of the ultimate sort of trouble a poor country boy can find himself in when he ventures into the big city. I'll take this over a batch of sappy love songs any day. The vocals are just right--emotional and seemingly heart felt as opposed to being maudlin or overly gushy. Even though this pre-dates his association with crackerjack songwriter Shel Silverstein, this is the album that declared Bobby Bare a long term force to be reckoned with on country music's turf.

CHARLIE DANIELS BAND "Fire on the Mountain" (1974) Kama Sutra. LP.

Get ready to toss this book across the room, Americana-hippies. In my opinion, country music as attempted by California style classic rock bands sucked. The harmonies were all wrong for openers. Yeah, yeah, lots of the musicians paid lip service to the obvious country legends. Unfortunately, with few exceptions they poorly interpreted country music adding their own shtick in the process. The results usually sound as bad as a chicken fried steak battered in granola would taste.

On the other hand, most southern rock bands such as the Charlie Daniels unit handled their country-ish songs with the respect they'd reserve for Grandpa's hunting rifle. It's plain to me that most of the southern boys were raised on Hank and the Opry whereas Left Coasters (including myself) didn't have the advantages of a good southern upbringing.

Some of the songs on this album aren't country influenced in the least. The few that are make this a must have album. "Long Haired Country Boy" is a table-thumping anthem for rednecks with hair who love the old ways, but also appreciate good weed along with their Jim Beam and like to crank their Marshall amps to 10. It's extremely important that visiting yankees understand the southern ways this song expresses, so well before venturing to Dixie, or someone might need to swiftly educate them on the spot in some juke joint.

The other crucial song is "The South's Gonna Do It" which is a nod to all the other major southern rock bands of the day. It's plainly influenced by the country king pins who'd salute each other in songs all the time, such as in Red Sovine's "Freightliner Fever."

"Trudy" and "Georgia" are both fine songs with one foot in country that are steeped in southern pride. Both songs seem lyrically wary of the hazards of venturing away too far from the south and home.

The final song on the LP is a hot version of "Orange Blossom Special" that features wild fiddlin' by Charlie himself. I'm sure that Roy Acuff would find something to bitch about, like the fact that a drum kit is used and the band was a bunch of longhairs, but to hell with him.

Today, Charlie Daniels has of course been with the Opry for many years and is considered as country as anybody else. This is obviously one of the milestone records that launched his career.

CHARLEY PRIDE "There's a Little Bit of Hank in Me" (1980) RCA. LP.

A lot of singers have tackled the task of recording a Hank William's Sr. tribute album over the years; Roy Acuff, Johnny Cash, etc. This is clearly one of the absolute best. Side one starts off with the title song, which was written especially for this occasion. It's a loving tribute that doesn't try to over deify Hank or get too maudlin. You might say that's the formula at work here. Let Charley's world-class voice carry the project. He gets right to work with "My Son Calls Another Man Daddy." Yeah Charley! What a voice. Hank would be tickled pink. On with standards like "A Mansion on the Hill" "I Can't Help It (If I'm Still In Love With You) and a couple that rarely get covered "Low Down Blues" and "I Could Never Be Ashamed of You."

The arrangements are very tasteful for an album released as late as 1980 and they sound well thought out as opposed to lots of other loving tributes I've heard that were slapped together. A few Hank purists probably don't like this album one bit. So what! Thee Whiskey Rebel does. If Hank were alive in 1980 his albums would probably sound like this. If I were awarding stars he'd get *****. But, this is Hank being paid tribute to so I'll award whiskey shots. Charley takes home a half-gallon of Rebel Yell.

CONWAY TWITTY'S "Greatest Hit's" (1960) MGM. LP.

Country purists may complain at the inclusion of this album because Mr. Twitty obviously still had one foot in rock and roll when he recorded these sides for MGM. I say so what? Even with his fabulous voice he probably seemed like a hick to lots of urban rock and roll fans. Forget his short term rock and roll image, Conway Twitty was as country as the "Twittyburger" recipe on the back of the album jacket. Included here is my all-time favorite ballad, "Lonely Blue Boy" during which Conway croaks like a bullfrog in heat between phrases. I've heard rumors over the years that Conway's "Mona Lisa" arrangement was… uhh… stolen from Carl Mann during a visit Conway made to Sun Records studio during a Mann recording session. Even if it was, Conway's strong vocals are far, far removed from Carl's boyish charms. There's plenty of room on anybody's record shelf for both. "It's Only Make Believe" is a timeless classic of course that builds in intensity as the song goes in a way that tells me that Harold Jenkins (real name--nobody on earth is named Twitty for real) listened to a lot of smooth early '50's R&B on the radio growing up in Friar's Point, Mississippi. When it's time for the old cornball Irish tune "Danny Boy" Conway really shines. He croons the first verse so pretty and sweet that he blows Elvis away at his own game; then to rub the King's face in his armpit he suddenly switches gears and the old stale square ballad becomes a red-hot rocker complete with more of his trademark intense croaking.

"COUNTRY MUSIC SALUTES the ARMED FORCES"

A titanic collection of twenty-four songs, that comes with a bizarre statement of purpose on the back cover. Evidently, the CMA, to help build the old hall of fame museum sponsored this album. For this purpose the notes state that the performers and songwriters all waived their royalties. Ok...fine. Now where in the hell does the armed forces fit in? Just how are they saluted? Certainly not by the choice of songs which are a mixed bag of topnotch classics.

Folks, you'd best call your neighbors on the telephone and tell them this LP is an extravaganza. We've got Hank Sr. singing: "Your Cheatin' Heart" Patsy Cline's "I fall To Pieces" Porter Wagoner's "Green Green Grass of Home" Bob Wills "San Antonio Rose" Hank Thompson's "The Green Light" and Johnny Cash's "Busted." Also heard are: Roy Acuff, Kitty Wells, Merle Travis, Jim Reeves and (amongst all these dignified treasures sung by legends) Billy Edd Wheeler chips in with his salute to the shit house "Ode to the Little Brown Shack" performed live no less.

If our house burned down tomorrow (knock on wood) with all our money in it and I had to start from scratch looking for vinyl to entertain myself in whatever dump we wound up living in, I'd start out with a cheap thrift store thirty-year old radio shack stereo and then go hit the dollar bins at the local record stores. They're full of albums like this. That's why the USA is the greatest country on earth. Our access to good cheap vinyl country LPs exceeds that of any other nation on the planet.

DON GIBSON "I Wrote a Song" (1963) RCA. LP.

I'm a real sucker for albums in which legendary songwriters sing their own material. This LP is a fine example why. "Oh Lonesome Me" has been sung by a score of huge well-known artists and about half the local honky tonk bands in the US. It's fun to hear Mr. Gibson's authoritative rendition. Likewise for "I Can't Stop Loving You" which to me is clearly performed and arranged better here than Ray Charles mega hit version. This album can't go wrong packed with so much great material including: "Lonesome Number One" "Give Myself a Party" and "A Legend in My Time." Even though Anita Kerr's trademark sticky-sweet, slick background vocal arrangements sound awful on some old RCA albums from the early '60's, she gets a thumbs up in this particular case along with head honcho producer Chet Atkins.

EDDY ARNOLD "A Dozen Hits" (1956) LP. RCA.

With all due respect, I'm usually not wild about Eddy Arnold's music. Why? To say Arnold's music over the years is "sedate" is an understatement. Gospel music of the era by the Blackwood Brothers or Red Foley is pure bedlam by comparison. What the hell, even though his music for the most part puts me to sleep there have always been millions of listeners who prefer soft, calmative music. Arnold was a huge commercial success. The back of the album liner notes refers to Eddy as being "America's first all-market vocalist" and as having a voice that is "polished in accent." Mr. Arnold served as a summer replacement on TV for of all people Perry Como who has to be one of the all-time most boring singers.

Having said all that, this particular album is chock full of pep. It manages to do what many an Arnold album has failed to do and that is to keep my toe tapping and my eyelids from rolling shut. There's a formula at work here: one song for each year from 1944-1955 is covered. 1955's "Sixteen Tons" features such a cool '50's-ish guitar squiggle that it alone makes this album worth owning. The great git-fiddle work doesn't end there. The album is full of it. "So Round So Firm So Fully Packed" from 1947, is flat-out fun to listen to and definitely not the sort of song a Perry Como audience would approve of. 1951's Hank tune "Cold Cold Heart" is well sung with a lot of feeling. "Slowpoke" (1952) Spade Cooley's "Shame on You" (1945) and a song that was picked up by Elvis himself later "A Fool Such As I" (1953) are amongst my other favorites here.

FREDDIE HART "The Neon and the Rain" (1960's) Kapp Records. LP.

A concept album loosely defined of heartache and split-up songs. "If You Ever Want to Kill Me" and "When Passion Commands" are earthy songs that stack up damned well with George Jones material from the same period. I'm a sucker for versions of the "I-got-the-last-laugh-on-that-bitch" classic "Cold Hard Facts of Life" and Freddie pulls it off well. The title track "The Neon and the Rain" is clearly the best song of the bunch. It's loaded with sordid lines that make me picture Freddie sitting in his car waiting outside a by the hour motel with a piece ready to get even. This album is definitely worth owning. Don't let the back cover liner notes mislead you: "a tender story of a broken romance." HAH! It's a lot more exciting and intense than that. It's only a notch or so shy of Johnny Paycheck's definitive Little Darlin' label cheatin' songs.

GARY STEWART "Out of Hand" (1975) RCA. LP.

As real country music cruised along through the mid-'70's on a collision course with the tasteless jackass label heads who took over in the '80's, Gary Stewart was one of the young studs working his way up the ladder. When George Jones sang "Who's Gonna Fill Their Shoes," well, here's one of the guys who was ready to do so. If things had worked out differently within the music biz he'd probably be living out the elder statesman role today that he so richly deserves. Instead, he records for independent labels and sings authentic country music to a loyal but smaller crowd while the hunks and divas thrive on the charts. What I personally dig about Gary Stewart (and I know quite a few fanatics who'll agree with me) is his knack for drinking songs of which there are two on this his debut album that without argument are worth taping and playing in your pickup truck as you cruise around knocking back cans of PBR "Drinkin' Thing" and "She's Acting Single (I'm drinking doubles)." The whole album is worth playing actually because it avoids boring, trite relationship songs with sappy words in favor of meaty tunes about people who like to (in the immortal words of G.G. Allin) "Drink Fight and Fuck." Although he's gone on to realize a healthy degree of success, in a perfect world Gary Stewart would've gone on to enjoy the recognition guys like Conway Twitty and George Jones have received.

George Jones "By Request" Epic Records. LP.

A collection of ten tunes recorded by Ol' Possum between 1981-1984, a tiny chunk of George's career; but just the tunes included here stack up against a peck of country artists career retrospective collections. Even though his personal memories may be a bit foggy from that time period, the early '80's were damn fine years for George music wise.

Stubborn traditionalists in some circles for his elaborate studio techniques have bellyached about his long-term legendary producer Billy Sherrill. His work shines here though from stem to stern. It probably wasn't exactly a teddy bear's goddamned picnic dealing with Jones during these years in the studio. I think B.S. watched his back damn well. The bone chilling slide guitar passages mixed front and center on "Still Doin' Time" perfectly match George's voice and help create one of the most graphic and desperate ever. I bet it was Billy who called for the strip club trumpet solo in one of two top-notch duets with Merle Haggard included here, "C.C. Water back." I've got to also single out "Tennessee Whiskey" which is my kind of love song. It's steeped in booze/love-oriented analogies from start to finish. The perfect closer for this batch is a lighthearted duet with the genius Ray Charles appropriately titled "We Didn't See a Thing." George and Ray sound like they're laughing their asses off throughout.

GEORGE JONES "24 greatest hits" Teevee Records CD

This CD is tailored perfectly to compliment the collection of folks (like myself) who have ample recordings already of George's Billy Sherrill produced period and his best known early stuff like "White Lightning" "Root Beer" "Why Baby Why" etc.

This isn't really his greatest twenty-four songs; it's just the greatest twenty-four songs this label licensed to sell. That's just fine with me. There are so damn many George Jones vinyl LPs available from different labels and so many of them repackage the same handful of songs over and over (sometimes with poor fidelity) that it's best in my humble opinion to have a couple CD's handy when a Jone's moment is at hand. I might add that usually it's about 6:30 in the morning and I've drank all night when I'm in the mood to listen to him. For some reason I don't listen to truck driving songs or obscure bar bands when the paperboy has already made the rounds. I want George or Hank Sr. or Porter to cap off my night. That's a piss poor time to be fumbling around with valuable out of print albums.

All these songs were released between 1961 and 1971. Some huge hits are included "She Thinks I Still Care" "I'll Share My World With You" and "Tender Years" are three of his absolute best songs as well as being amongst his best known. I'm also extremely partial to "Things Have Gone to Pieces" (which is along the lines of the later "These Days I Barely Get By") a fantastic cheating song "Tell Me My Lying Eyes Are Wrong" and a great hard luck story song that only hit number 28 "Where Grass Won't Grow."

Don't be like the snobs who might fret over this CD because it's on the "TeeVee" label instead of a big major. Keep your precious Jones albums on the shelf and keep your hands free for pouring drinks and chain smoking. Take it easy though! Twenty-four straight tracks of Jones is a strong dose. Don't plan on driving immediately afterwards.

GEORGE JONES "Anniversary" (1982) Epic Label. CD.

If I was allowed free reign to assemble a "greatest hits" of George Jones material he'd definitely have an album you'd need to slap a warning sticker on. This 22-song collection represents merely his first 10 years of recording with Billy Sherrill (1972-1982). It's finest moments are as emotionally gripping as just about anything recorded in the country music genre.

"These Days I Barely Get By" which is a song plainly written for losers everywhere to identify with, is so sad it'd make a wino wince. "He Stopped Loving Her Today" is an absolute classic of course, delivered masterfully by George who was going through a living hell battling the demons in his own life at the time. "If Drinkin' Don't Kill Me (Her Memory Will)" and "Still Doin' Time" are just friggin' over the top hardcore scenarios depicting real life chronic alcoholism as both a cause and effect of a shattered relationship. Just like so much great music covered in this book, these songs are brilliant and timeless because they can be understood and recognized as the ugly, I repeat: U-G-L-Y goddamned truth by "the people" ranging from hard luck poverty stricken folks who can barely read to urban egghead critics studying the words and enunciation.

"The Grand Tour" also deserves special mention as a classic example of George's ability to sell a tragic song in an icy detached manner rather than resort to gratuitous studio histrionics.

GEORGE JONES "Sings Country & Western Hits" Mercury Records. LP.

This album features some of ol' Possum's absolute best early '60's songs of despair. The liner notes on the back cover spend a lot of time carefully explaining why George is the logical heir to Hank Williams Sr. musically speaking. I can dig that when for proof we've got songs like the jealous and miserable "Window Up Above" and George's "Just One More" which is neck deep in the sort of authentic alcoholic misery that ol' Hank expressed so well. "Life To Go" which George wrote sure as hell doesn't lighten the mood any. Hank would sure as hell recognize a kindred spirit in George. I betcha he'd laugh as hard as I did at the irony of him singing "I Walk the Line" on side two.

Lots of classics are included as well in this full to the brim album such as "Heartaches By the Number" "Oh Lonesome Me" and (another Brother of the bottle) Lefty Frizzell's; "If You've Got the Money, I've Got the Time."

GEORGE JONES "Where Grass Won't Grow" Musicor Records.

A nice bunch of melancholy songs spear headed by the first rate title track. The material isn't over the top tragic like so many other Jones albums, nor is it peppered with novelty songs. There's not a drinking song to be found here either. I guess you could say this album is best suited for George's large contingent of non-honky tonkin' "square" fans. You don't have to be a cube to enjoy it though. "For Better or For Worse (But Not For Long)" is a dandy number. "Until I Remember You're Gone" "No Blues Is Good News" and "Same Old Boat" are all fine songs. Don't let it upset you that these cuts wouldn't offend your clergyman or your Grandma. Just spin the album, feel a couple tiny tears welling up, but instead of hitting the jug, heat up a cup of hot milk and call it a night early.

JACK GREENE "There Goes My Everything" (1966) Decca. LP.

Image has always been very important to country singers. Some of the more suave fellas like Conway Twitty or Slim Whitman seem to be loaded with sex appeal. On the other hand there's guys like Dick Curless or Dave Dudley or Waylon who look like they could kick your ass. Then there's the sometimes out of control emotional honky tonk singers like Hank Sr. or George Jones. If you judge by this record, Jack Greene's first album, you'd think that Nashville had found a perfect niche for him all of his own as a guy whose always getting dumped by women, always "Almost Persuaded" as opposed to going all the way, always sustaining "A Wound Time Can't Erase." Jack never fights back on this album, instead he declares "I Think I'll Go Somewhere and Cry Myself to Sleep."

Here's some more song titles from this album, see if you can notice the pattern: "The Hurts on Me" "Ever Since My Baby Went Away" and "Make the World Go Away".

Even the great Johnny Ray occasionally sang a few happy tunes; occasionally he didn't get dumped or mistreated in a song. But Jack Greene never once cries in his beer at a tavern or walks the streets combing the smoke filled honky tonks for his round-heeled gal. He waits for her to come back when she's tired of more exciting men and wants a man who can cook and vacuum for her.

I just wish once in this nice collection of songs Jack would either cheat in return or haul off and bitch slap his latest Delilah.

But of course, that would ruin the album for all the middle of the road milk-toast type country fans that sympathize with guys who are doormats for dominant women.

What the hell, at least he's got a woman to dump him in every song. That's more than a lot of guys have going for them.

JERRY REED'S "RCA Collectors Series" (1985) LP .

Holy crap! Jerry Reed is an incredible talent. Side two is flawless, seven songs in a row of great material. "East Bound & Down" finds me climbing on the table. "When You're Hot You're Hot" finds me doing the boogaloo stark naked with a jug of Beam in one hand and a six-pack in the other. "I'm Just a Redneck in a Rock and Roll Bar" is unique and brilliant. I've emptied most of the alcohol into my system by now; "Amos Moses" is on and my wife's getting concerned. "Patches" has me crying in my beer." My wife now knows for sure I've flipped. "She Got the Goldmine (I Got the Shaft)" may be the best divorce song ever. My wife has tuned me out completely. She's watching the Andy Griffith show, how appropriate. The final track on side two "The Bird," has left me in an Otis-the-Drunk like state. I'm too sauced to flip the album over. If I keep trying I'm gonna wind up playing side three. Well what the hell, this one qualifies for this book based on side two. I'm sure the more straight earlier songs from Jerry's career sound just fine.

JIM ED BROWN "Bottle Bottle" RCA. LP.

When you go over hundreds and hundreds of country albums with a fine tooth comb a few patterns begin to emerge that one might not spot even through years of casual listening. For instance, a big selling legend passes away and a year or two or three later a fresh artist bearing a vague resemblance to the sorely missed superstar is given a big push. Maybe it's just the Lone Star and Jim Beam I'm sucking down as I listen to this album and gaze at the pictures, but I'll be damned if ol' Jim Ed Brown doesn't seem to come across like a more two-fisted version of the late great RCA crooner Jim Reeves. Jim Ed's pop music gig with The Browns had certainly seen better days this many years into the '60's. This album with these high quality smooth songs seems like a nice way to repackage his velvet voice. I don't mean to blaspheme Jim Reeves who in spite of his knack for wearing soft sweaters to photo shoots was a rugged ball player and one of popular music's great voices.

Being honest though, with Dean Martin wearing the crooner crown with a "10" voice… I'd give Jim Reeves an "8" and Jim Ed Brown an "8.5." The title song is one of the finest odes to the bottle ever written. The first words were crafted carefully to deceive listeners into thinking the singer was pressing his lips to those of a tender gal… HAH! The song unfolds into a love poem to a partner who'll never turn on a fella. Another stand out is Mr. Brown laying down the law to his spouse with "I'll Make the Living". The pre-Freddy Fender reading of "Before the Next Teardrop Falls" rates high as well.

JOHNNY HORTON "Greatest Hits" (1961) Columbia Records

"The Battle of New Orleans," wasn't just a hit song, it was a damned event. Of course, If It was new today it wouldn't be played even once on the air. It's just too wordy and indelicate by modern standards. Of course back in Horton's heyday TV Western's were popular instead of hokey reality shows with no plot designed for today's viewers with poor attention spans. The best of the songs on this LP are all two fisted and manly, which means they'd also be considered politically incorrect these days. "Jim Bridger" suggests that we knock back a shot of booze in salute to a great ol' mountain man. "Johnny Reb" points out the positive aspects of CSA soldiers. "Spring time in Alaska" involves gunplay in a remote Alaska setting, where miners are unabashedly disrupting the ecological balance. And "Sink the Bismarck" would likely bring about a sanction from the U.N. if it were released today.

I'm glad Johnny Horton was alive when he was and never had to witness cool songs like these sneered at by a nation of Oprah fans. Happily this album has been in print for so many years in various formats that the sensitivity police will never be able to seize all our copies!!

JOHNNY RUSSELL "Rednecks White Socks & Blue Ribbon Beer" RCA Records. LP

This is sure as hell one of those albums that could qualify for a book like this based on the strength of one big title song. This was Russell's first album ever and I suppose he could've wound up classified with the one hit wonders if he didn't have more going for him, but he did. He sings on this LP with the soulfulness of a Bobbie Gentry and a big voice that stacks up with those of legends (check out his version of Conway Twitty's "You've Never Been This Far Before"). Johnny's voice is a very subtle tool when the situation calls for it on ironic songs like "Finer Things in Life" and "Making Plans." But, like the legends I referred to earlier he can give voice to what the masses feel but cannot express on their own in songs such as the title track and side two's "Drinkin' Beer and Singing a Country Song."

The RCA folks must've known Johnny was a keeper in terms of having long range potential. The session musicians provided are first class. The cover of this album is one of my absolute favorites. It shows the rather rotund Mr. Russell sitting at a table in a bar with a bunch of regular Joe hardhats. He's picking and grinning for them and there's a pile of dead cans in the middle of the table. It perfectly depicts middle America in 1973. "Rednecks White Socks and Blue Ribbon Beer" is an anthem of the people and to this day it receives a rousing chorus of rebel yells and waved fists when played on jukeboxes in blue-collar taverns across the USA.

KENNY PRICE "Southern Bound" (1967) Boone Records. LP.

A grinning Kenny (the "round mound of sound") sports a cool looking purple suit on the front cover of this album as he is shown hoisting a thumb over his shoulder to hitch a ride. The back cover has four more pictures of Kenny with a tiny little suitcase still looking for a ride back down to Dixie one presumes. I'd like to think that the suitcase is full of copies of this topnotch album for the folks back home rather than undershorts and a toothbrush.

I dunno why Boone Records didn't buy him a bus ticket, but lets face it they were a small label. Presuming all this actually happened, when he eventually got back home I bet his family was tickled pink and double proud to hear Kenny's voice booming out songs of the road like "Southern Bound" "Yonder Comes a Freight Train" and the Hank Cochran penned "I'm a Long Way from Home." I've got to quibble with the positive slant assumed about one of my least favorite cities: "Downtown Knoxville" but this album is so heavy with great material not worked to death elsewhere I'll overlook that. On side two, right about where the filler material sits on most country albums we're treated to the worthy "Grass Don't Grow on a Busy Street" and "My Goal for Today." I wonder what the folks back home thought of Kenny's incredibly cool purple suit?

Little JIMMY DICKENS "Greatest Hits" Columbia Records. LP.

If Mr. Dickens has ever had a booze or drug problem or has had women trouble we'd never know from his music. That isn't to say that Jimmy Dickens songs are dull or goody goody. This collection is packed with songs that would most appeal to country folks who can identify with the subject matter. For example: "A-Sleepin' at the Foot of the Bed" and "Take An Old Cold Tater and Wait." Both songs might make little sense to suburban kids these days brainwashed by MTV. Even though Jimmy didn't write 'em, you'd swear he lived both songs out as a child.

If almost any other country legend hit the radio with, "Truck Load of Starvin' Kangaroos" the fans would think they were nuts, but it's just Little Jimmy Dickens style. His biggest hit of course was “May the Bird of Paradise Fly Up Your Nose” which harkens back to the good old days when wacky novelty tunes would be played by both country and pop DJs. Jimmy can sing straight songs just fine too. “Fireball Mail” and “Wabash Cannonball” a nice change of pace on side two. The LP is wrapped up with Jimmy wavin’ goodbye with the homespun: “You All Come.” May the bird of paradise crap on your droopy hip-hop pants if you don’t dig Jimmy Dickens!

MEL TILLIS “Who’s Julie?” (late ‘60’s) Kapp Records. LP.

The gods that burdened Mel with a stutter also blessed him with a warm, endearing singing voice that stacks up with the Porters and Farons of his generation. This album is an excellent demonstration of Mel’s versatility. It starts off with a couple standards: “My Special Angel” and “Detroit City” (which he wrote) and eventually winds its way into the honky tonk realm with the joyfully pathetic “Sorrow Overtakes the Wine” and the rowdy “Love Ain’t Gonna Die (I’m Gonna Have To Kill it). The album ending “Ballad of Forty Dollars,” is a twisted graveyard humor song written by the sometimes maniacal, Tom T. Hall. For those who are keeping track there is no filler on this album whatsoever. I might add there are no hokey gimmicks used in the production of these songs unlike some albums from this era that seemed to be attempts to compete with experimental rock and roll albums. Just good straight forward country music from a true pro.

"The MERLE TRAVIS Guitar" (1956) Capitol Records. LP.

This is thee traditional country guitar textbook album. There are no vocals, even though Merle was an accomplished singer. There is no band. There is just the master and his Gibson guitar. We are treated to a variety of twelve tunes at close quarters by the grand potentate of country pickers. Like myself, most guitar players I've known over the years couldn't even attempt to hope to emulate one of the simpler songs on this LP badly without a few years of serious lessons. Even the guys I know for whom the guitar is an extension of their arms shake their heads in awe when Professor Travis kicks it into high gear on numbers like: "Rockabye Rag" "Walkin' the Strings" and "Blue Smoke" You need to be born with the talent to play like this. Merle Travis has inspired as many country and rockabilly guitar players as Hank Sr. inspired singers. He was to country guitar playing in the latter half of the 20th century what Jimi Hendrix was to the rock and roll genre. All that talent, plus he composed "Sixteen Tons."

NAT STUCKEY "New Country Roads" (1969) LP. RCA.

Nat Stuckey "does his thing" in true '60's fashion. He tackles pop songs like the futuristic "In the Year 2525," originally recorded by label mates Zager and Evans and CCR's "Bad Moon Rising." I doubt he drew many hippies or rock fans to his shows as a result of this rock concept platter. He sings utilizing his strong voice well, but pronounces the words a little bit too clearly and, maybe a bit stiffly. You could even say he sounds a little bit like a square trying hard to be hip. Well, maybe a bit more than just a little.

The electric guitars on "Roll Over Beethoven" might have scared off Jack Webb types in 1969, but little else would have. In spite of the fact that this album may not have endeared Nat to the Woodstock set in the late '60's, I still enjoy the hell out of this. It's fun to listen to from a nostalgic, semi-serious standpoint, undoubtedly more fun than it was to feast your ears upon it back in the day. Nat's reading of the old classic: "Cut Across Shorty" with it's blandly asinine lyrics is given a dramatic interpretation perhaps worthy of William Shatner's finest recorded works from the same period. The Boxtop's hit "The Letter" is crooned by Nat so intensely that you forget it's just a silly top-40 pop hit. Bottom line, what we have here is a twisted country classic.

THE PO' BOYS (Bill Anderson Presents) s/t (1968) Decca Records. LP.

A long heralded country tradition is the gung ho way that backing bands for stars jump into the breech to keep the crowd busy when said star is shit faced drunk backstage or AWOL. The Po' Boys turn in such a fine performance here that I suspect I might enjoy a live set of theirs as much if not better than a Bill Anderson set. That's no slight to Mr. Anderson who is a great songwriter and singer in his own right. It's just that I'm a sucker for steel guitar and fiddle instrumentalists and there are one apiece worth writing home about in his band.

Texas's own Weldon Myrick is a crackerjack steel guitar man. He's featured here in "Corn Crib" "No More Money No More Honey" and a slick interpretation of "Beautiful

Dreamer." Fiddler Jimmy Gateley shows his stuff on "Orange Blossom Special" and "Maiden's Prayer." I could sit and enjoy either one of those guys for three sets in my local tavern any day of the week. Guitar player Jim Lance is the focal point of a couple songs too: "Dear Heart" and "Yellow Bird." Drummer Len Miller shows he's not "just a drummer" by crooning: "Let Me Talk to You."

Bill Anderson's band was well endowed with talent back in those days. I can only think of a few other bands that can hold the spotlight as effectively and you can bet they're all somewhere here in this book.

PORTER WAGONER "The Cold Hard Facts of Life" (1967) RCA Records. LP.

To dedicated Elvis Presley fans, following the King goes beyond merely listening to music and watching movies once in a while--it becomes a full-fledged hobby. The same can be said about Porter Wagoner. His career is long enough and fruitful enough to fill twenty-five hours per week. Bluegrass albums, country albums, psychotic/drinking song concept albums, live offerings, hundreds of hours of TV footage and a slew of Porter/Dolly duets. Before he passed, he evidently was a greeter sometimes at Opryland. He stayed busy and as a result there's plenty to sink your teeth into when it comes to ol' Porter.

The Cold Hard Facts of Life, album is an amazing cultural artifact with songs that rack up a huge box score of killings, threats, tragic deaths, busted lives and even an occasional spirit that will not bend. The cover shows Porter standing at his front door, bowling bag in hand, apparently having just caught his wife turtle-doving with some dude on his couch. The guy's obviously reached first base. Porter's wife is trying to brush his hand off her boob.

According to Wagoner's biographer the cover shot was taken at the apartment Porter took after suffering through a split with his real wife (the 'neck on the couch is part of the RCA sound crew). The cover shot is a much softer take on the actual conclusion of the title song, which ends in a double knife killing. Usually mild mannered Bill Anderson, who also contributes the equally morbid, penned the song: "The First Mrs. Jones," which stars a psychotic wife killer. "Hundred Dollar Funeral" is a morbid testimony to the ultimate emptiness of the end of a human life complete with gothic church organ and the Anita Kerr singers warbling sadly in the background.

Porter's voice is masterful and as soothing as actor Vincent Price's throughout while delivering a roster of songs that might be considered mere exploitation numbers if sang by a lesser talent. Indeed, I've heard a half dozen other versions of "Cold Hard Facts" from the '60's by other talented country singers that seem awkward and second rate compared to Porter's. This is a landmark album for the thin man from West Plains even when judged against the rest of his best work.

PORTER WAGONER "Confessions of a Broken Man" (1966) RCA. LP.

How many damn Porter albums do I own? I lost count around forty or so. With only one or two exceptions they are all fine, fine records. He had an amazingly consistent career since he started out in 1953. This album though stands out in several ways. Porter went out of his way to conduct research for this one. He actually bought a suit of raggedy clothes and headed to skid row in Nashville to check out the "cruel tragic realities of life" (I quote the back cover liner notes). His trip to the row was quite fruitful. This album is part of an ambitious trilogy of 1960's "hard living" albums along with two drinking song oriented masterpieces, which were recorded in the same time period that you can read about elsewhere in this book.

Porter's delivery of tragic songs like "Skid Row Joe" and "I Just Came to Smell the Flowers" is icy cold. He chills you to the bone as opposed to more tearful, maudlin renditions of tragic songs by fellow masters Red Sovine and Hank Williams Sr. That's not to deprecate their superb material. Porter Wagoner is simply unique stylistically. When he emotes: "How Far Down Can I Go?" and "My Last Two Tens" he's not just going through the usual motions at some Nashville session. Damn it, he understood these, "Men With Broken Hearts."

Porter spent the bulk of his career both before and after his "wino trilogy" period presenting himself as a slick master of ceremony's dressed in flashy Nudie suits. There are no light-hearted bluegrass heel hoppers or pleasant novelty numbers to be heard here, though. The bums in these songs aren't happy hobos, instead they are the fellows who drink Sterno and freeze to death in lonely alleys. Porter doesn't ruin the songs with political rhetoric like ol' Woody Guthrie or "concerned" folk singers of his own era; instead he asks that we try to simply understand these fellows and realize that they aren't monsters. They once were just like us with homes, relationships and credit cards run up past their limit.

Porter Wagoner "Soul of a Convict" (1967) RCA. LP

I just love Porter's concept albums. This one closely follows a "prison song" theme right down to a couple photos showing Porter posing in a real live cell decked out in a pair of striped prison pajamas.

The album begins with the snappy rhythm of the semi humorous "Boston Jail." The happy mood factor goes straight down the seatless, soiled prison crapper from there. "I Relived My Life Today" is a sad reflection on happier times that Porter really gets into. It's enough to wipe the smile off ones face instantly like a sudden lap full of scalding hot coffee. It was written by the great, Vic McAlpin, who sold Porter a lot of songs over the years. "Let Me In," features seemingly the same son of an alky kid from, "One Dime for Wine." Side two provides a fine home for Porter's stellar version of: "Green Green Grass of Home." He wraps the project up with an extremely tasteful and all too rarely covered Hank Williams Sr. lament "(I Heard That) Lonesome Whistle."

Obviously, Porter didn't have as deep an understanding of convicts as his peers Johnny Cash and Merle Haggard had, but he did his best and managed to come up with a great album anyway.

PORTER WAGONER "The bottom of the Bottle" (1968) RCA. LP.

Being the number one drinking song "theme" album of all time, this has to be considered one of the lynchpin LPs in all of country music history. Porter researched long and hard before recording this and the two other albums that make up his wino trilogy. He actually went to the trouble of dressing up and tramping skid row a few times in the clothes you see him wearing inside the bottle the sober Porter on the cover is peering into.

I think Porter's studies led him to two conclusions. First, we should pity the fellows who wind up on the row--they're only human--it could happen to anybody. Secondly, uhh... yeah... there is a good deal of comfort to be found from a bottle. This LP is as much a concept album as rock albums like "Ziggy Stardust and the Spiders from Mars" and "Tommy." It starts off with a philosophical narration entitled "The Wino" complete with tinkling bottles in the alley sounds in the background. One line speculates: "could it be that he loved and lost... or that he was lost and unloved?" This bit of sympathy conditions the listener to not prejudge the drunks Porter's about to sing about. "Daddy and the Wine" is a homey tale of a neglected motherless kid who's "on the candy" since his daddy's been "on the wine."

Three Merle Haggard drinking song classics are used here to fine effect: "Swinging Doors" "I Threw Away the Rose" and the anthem: "Tonight the Bottle Let Me Down." Harlan Howard's: "She Burnt the Little Roadside Tavern Down" is a horrifying tale of a MADD mother type gone berzerk. Of course, psuedo-moralistic songs like, "Wine" and "Bottle Bottle" both make me yearn to drink rather than turn over a new leaf. Hell, you can say that about the whole album. That's the bottom line why it's worth finding at any price!

PORTER WAGONER "The Farmer" (1973) RCA. LP.

One of the reasons so many Porter Wagoner albums are so great is the fact that he doesn't do things the easy way like so many performers. For example, at some point when this album was conceived he didn't simply send the RCA folks a request for all the farm oriented numbers they could dig up to re-hash. He wrote nine out of ten of these songs! The exception is a fine nostalgic Dolly song "Daddy's Work Boots."

Porters title track "The Farmer" is a big ol' two-fisted salute that sounds like it's really from his heart. "My Dad" and "Moments of Meditation" could play on radio stations that program sacred music. Later on side two, things liven up a lot though, with a tale of an unwelcome skunk "Wake Up Jacob" followed later by a novelty song about a fellow with a knack for modern dance steps "Country Bo-Bo." The final song "Bones" has some adventurous production and percussive sounds that are pretty damned innovative for this genre of music. Like I said, Porter rarely did things the easy way. He seemed determined to create new sounds while keeping one foot firmly anchored in tradition.

PORTER WAGONER "Tore Down" (1974) RCA. LP.

This is a classic example of Porter's knack for cutting albums that brilliantly alternate between grim, violent songs and tunes so nauseatingly cheerful he had to be deliberately tinkering with his listeners minds. The title track "Tore Down" is a frank song about personally being in pain and broken down. The flip side to that one is the album ender "Happy Faces" which is an almost sickeningly optimistic song about being in some sort of jolly hellish place where everyone smiles.

"Graduation Day" seems like a sincere loving message to one of Porter's children, yet also included is one of Dolly Parton's infamous dead rube songs "Cassie." The absolute crowning moment heard on this twelve-incher is the triple schizo "George Leroy Chickashea" which Porter was so serious about molding into some sort of ultimate song that he actually commissioned an artist to paint "George." The character is third white, black and Indian. The tale of his hellish life is backed by fluttering musical snatches of wah-pedal, funk guitar, tom-toms and traditional country twang, that make for an irresistible but (let's face it) psychotic musical stew.

Rock and roll fans love to crow about the Beatles pulling off songs that aren't nearly as complex as this one. If you're a music fan you must hear "George Leroy Chickashea" at least once in your life or you're really missing out on something special.

PORTER WAGONER "What Ain't to be, Just Might Happen" (1972) RCA. LP.

This one is totally top heavy with side one busting at the seams at the expense of the flip side. Porter's concept this time around is mental health. The set opener title song is light hearted in a homespun philosophical way. It's immediately followed by a song about a town oddball who walks around wearing homemade shoes and clothing, yet turns out to be a wealthy man: "Waldo the Weirdo."

Next we come to the heart and soul of this fantastic album, which is as warped and spooky as the distorted mirrors in your local funhouse; "The Rubber Room." It's without a doubt one of the absolute top achievements creatively speaking of Mr. Wagoner's long, long career. Producer Bob Ferguson makes incredibly shocking use of an echo effect. Porter's vocal work on this one rises above even the alarming special effects. Obviously long-term country superstars like Porter were aware of all the heavily produced concept albums rock and roll artists had been making for years. I can imagine fellows like John Lennon and Frank Zappa and Brian Wilson listening to "The Rubber Room" and being blown away!

Side one ends with "If I Lose My Mind" which is terrifying as well and "Comes and Goes" which features a cool swirly musical arrangement meant to signify, periodic insanity. Side two is almost better left un-discussed. It's not awful, but it seems rather mundane after side one. The songs are of the everyday optimistic country sort.

The superb steel guitar work by the legendary Pete Drake on side one deserves special mention. At some points (such as the reading of Waldo's will) he's virtually the only musical accompaniment to Porters voice.

ROY CLARK "The Best of" (1960's) Dot Records. LP.

There's absolutely no doubt that Roy Clark oozes with talent. In my book he'd be immortal merely from his appearances on The Beverly Hillbillies, not to mention his Hee Haw years, and the years in between in which he was most often heard singing commercial pop-country on the radio, that was a far cry from the traditional picking a lot of us associate him with.

This album mostly features his most popular songs from his violin saturated pop phase. You could say in fact that

"Yesterday When I Was Young" is the extreme border of how commercial and string drenched a song can be and still gain my approval for this book. It is a good song. Even though I rarely play it at home, when I hear it on the radio (it's a favorite on our local Texas classic country station) I always enjoy it.

"Thank God and Greyhound" is a brilliant song that starts off in a maudlin pop manner, but ends up shifting gears halfway through morphing into a joyous kiss off to a stifling relationship. "I Never Picked Cotton" is a brilliant song and the arrangement here is as strong as that of Johnny Cash's '90's version. Along with some other decent pop songs Roy and Dot Records, included the instrumental gem, "Malaguena" which is blisteringly good surf guitar pickin'. I wonder if this is where Junior Brown got the idea to include a surf medley on one of his albums?

STONEWALL JACKSON "Tribute to Hank Williams" (1960's) Columbia Records. LP.

I've said it before and I'll say it again, when it comes to judging the plethora of Hank tribute albums my method is to focus on the lyrical passages where Hank himself really poured it on thick. He knew the strong points in his own songs and it sucks when either a simple local tavern cover band or a famous pop singer slides through one of those moments oblivious to the way Hank phrased the words himself.

Stonewall Jackson obviously understands Hanks songs. His voice interprets the lyrics like they should be interpreted. He "feels Hank's pain" to paraphrase a politician who'll remain nameless here. "A Mansion on the Hill" and "Let's

Turn Back the Years" (which just happen to be the last two songs on side two) seems to actually go above and beyond the call of duty in the sense that he reads meaning into the words beyond the original versions.

I really am impressed by the way he sets up the album with a loving tribute tune titled "Here's to Hank" then wades right into, "I'm So Lonesome I Could Cry" without any pause. The only disappointing thing about this LP is that Stonewall sings for the most part the same Hank classics covered on every other tribute; but even that's not really a bad thing when you think about it.

TENNESSEE ERNIE FORD "This Lusty Land" Capitol Records. LP.

A manly collection of songs that certainly is in the spirit of the macho flannel shirt ol' Ern's sporting on the cover. He's working exactly the same territory Johnny Cash did in his Western and folk music oriented concept albums. I'm not sure whose label decided to direct their singer to copy who, so lets keep this rivalry friendly.

Whereas Johnny overall pulls these sort of songs off just a bit better Ford is no slouch. The musical arrangements which are often lead by clarinets are very original and enjoyable as hell. While Cash is the master of sounding wired and parched and maybe just a wee bit loco singing period songs, Ford's voice is calm and cool and rich.

Ford's treatment of delicate ballads such as "Who Will Shoe Your Pretty Little Foot" and "In the Pines" is fantastic. He sounds relaxed and pleasantly down home. Very soothing. Picture yourself drinking a cool glass of buttermilk with Andy Griffith on his porch. His versions of "John Henry" and "Nine Pound Hammer" are great in their own right, although like I said before they're not quite up to the superstar standards of Cash.

TOM T. HALL "Country Is" (1974) Mercury Records. LP

Some country songwriters are fairly one dimensional, not so Tom T. Hall. Over the years he wrote a wide variety of songs ranging in mood from down right morbid to sticky sweet maudlin. This collection of songs, like most of his work is somewhere in the middle; "I Feel Like Flying Away" is incredibly upbeat, to the point of almost being disgusting as far as my personal tastes go. On the other hand "Canadian Women Canadian Clubs" makes me want to pour a drink for all the best reasons. "God Came Through Bellville Georgia" is flat-out strange, and "Going To Hell in a Basket" leaves me scratching my head in a happy way too. Mr. Hall's cover of "Over the Rainbow" fits the unpredictable pattern of this album. Don't fight this smorgasbord of sound, put a bit of everything on your plate. You're bound to find quite a bit to suit your taste here. Definitely a cut above run of the mill love song albums.

8. OBSCURE

BUZZ MARTIN "Where There Walks a Logger" Ripchord. LP.

The liner notes on the back of the album declare that Buzz is Oregon's answer to Grandpa Jones. With all due respect to Grandpa, Buzz Martin's voice and songs were much more along the lines of what you'd expect to hear from Johnny Cash. Even though Buzz may never have become very well known to folks in Tennessee or Texas, I have it on good authority that more often than not whenever Johnny passed through the Pacific Northwest he'd cover one of Buzz's songs live to pay his respects. For a significant part of his life Buzz Martin was a L-O-G-G-E-R and his songs were more often than not about his chosen trade. He possessed a voice that was nearly as endearing and warm as Johnny's and a knack for writing songs about the life of a logger that is to my knowledge unsurpassed in the entire realm of country music. Side one opens with a spoken piece with guitar in the background: "Used Log Truck" Buzz tells a story about a logger's rise and sad fall serving as his own boss, buying his own truck. "There Walks a Man" is the title track, a hard boiled insider's thumbnail sketch of what the average logger is all about. "Unemployment Compensation" is one song I'd have loved to hear Mr. Cash cover, maybe he did live. It's the sort of down to earth song that few singers can pull off. "Logger's Home Brew" is a catchy drinking song that makes my head ache. Damn, this simple logger wrote great songs. Incidentally, even though Buzz Martin was mainly known in his own neck of the woods during his lifetime, today I personally know of dedicated fans of his ranging from San Francisco to New York City to Germany and on to Australia. He was that good.

DEE MULLINS "The Continuing Story" (1969) Plantation Records. LP.

This album is obviously a Plantation Records attempt to get a rub off of the success of label mate Jeannie C. Riley's "Harper Valley PTA" for a male singer. The song isn't an answer or really much of a continuation for that matter. It's certainly not the song I like the best on this album even though it's penned by the great Tom T. Hall. My favorite is another song by Mr. Hall "Beers" which is a salute to the guy who used to sell he and his pals frosties when they were underage.

I also really like the attitude of the words and the squawk box talking steel guitar effect on "I Am the Grass." "Parking For Cheaters" is a well sung adultery oriented tune and "War

Baby" manages to comment on that little war that was in progress without going overboard either way. "The Big Man" would've made a helluva Dave Dudley song, Dee Mullins fills those shoes quite well though.

Judging by the album cover photos Dee appears to have patronized the same barber as Jack Lord. Wow! So why is this the only Dee Mullins LP listed in any of my guides? Did he get hit by a bus or get drafted? I want more!!

Don Lee "Dreams of the Everyday Housewife" Custom Records. LP.

This is an obscurity that most folks would probably flip past, in the dollar bin at the record store. Why? The cover doesn't reveal in anyway what a wild ride is in store for the listener. The front cover is just a picture of a blond lady grinning and holding a wooden spoon. The back cover is just generic info about other equally obscure label releases.

But, when you pop the needle on it's like walking into a small, seedy little lounge in the late '60's. The band is sitting in one corner of the room. Most of the patrons are ignoring them. The singer, who looks drunk as hell, is hunched over his keyboard snarling out a melancholy ballad about love gone wrong with a frown on his face. The tune ends, but the singer doesn't acknowledge the smattering of applause. He shrugs. (Hey, he's singing for himself. Fuck the audience he mumbles). He takes a hit off the bourbon and water at his elbow and hunches back over the piano into another bitter number. The three-piece backing band looks nervous. They seem intimidated by the singer as though he's a ticking alcoholic time bomb. They seem to be silently praying he won't go off on them or the audience. The set continues thus.

The songs are about as bitter as you're ever going to hear. Songs for the jilted, alky losers. Songs for the tired of living.

A little while before closing time a drunk lady in the back of the smoky room blurts out between songs: "HEY!! PLAY SOMETHING HAPPY for once!" The singer who is plowed by now shakes his head a bit and mutters something again under his breath. The band looks more worried than ever. They look at their wristwatches praying for closing time to come soon. The singer announces somberly into the mic: "here's a happy one lady" and tinkles out the opening notes of the saddest song in the bands songbook: "Name Of the Game." The song is simply too much for the small crowd of drinkers. None of them feel like partying listening to songs this sad. The bar is mostly cleared of customers twenty minutes before last call. The bartender thinks to himself, I gotta let these guys go.

EDDIE DEAN "A Tribute to Hank Williams" ('60's) LP

There's got to be a hundred different Hank tribute albums out there waiting to be dug out of the collective budget vaults of record stores in America. A book could practically be written purely on the subject of loving tributes to him. A veteran of the well known cowboy music combo "Riders of the Purple Sage" Mr. Dean's credentials are superb and his tribute to Hank is deserving of owning for sure. Actually about a half of this is Hank tunes and the other half a potpourri of filler songs including a couple gospel numbers my church going mom (who has always hated country music for being too secular) would really dig.

The Hank songs including: ”Hey Good Looking” “Cold Cold Heart” and “Baby We’re Really in Love” are well played and sung. Upon my first spin of this album I was sent scrambling for a pack of Q-Tips when I thought I heard a Hammond organ in the background. It turned out to actually be an organ, which made sense after I remembered that Hank was indeed also accompanied by them, on occasion (such as “Too Many Parties and Too Many Pals”). The non-religious filler tunes: “Boogie Woogie Cowboy” and “One Has My Name-One Has My Heart” are definitely worth a few listens too.

EDDY DRAKE “Country Sounds of Today” (1973) LP Newhall Records.

Another great unknown paladin of country music who deserved a longer contract with one of the big labels of the 1970’s. Eddy combines some of the best traits of Jerry Lee Lewis and King Elvis (when in his country mode) himself on this album. Each side begins with a popular well-known cover song “Promised Land” and “Proud Mary.” A lot of average local bar band types might also cover these songs being used to churning out four sets per night in honky tonks, but Eddy’s versions are as soulful and as solid in a swaggering way as you’d expect from the biggest name performers.

I’ll be damned if Eddy doesn’t breath new life into the old chestnut “Goodnight Irene” which I never really cared for until I heard this version. As for his original “I Had a Dream Last Night” and “Call Me in the Morning” both achieve solid B+ grades. Mr. Drakes band is staffed with great musicians including world-class guitarists James Burton and Al Casey.

The back cover liner notes are written by former Capitol records grand poohbah, Cliffie Stone who evidently produced this small label album at least in part. Evidently Drake released quite a few singles over the years. I guess I'm gonna have to chase 'em down.

FREDDY CARR "Freddy's Favorites" (1968) Del Records. LP.

His name isn't mentioned in three record guides and there's not a single mention of him on the Internet either. It may seem the world has forgotten ol' Freddy, but hey folks, I haven't. As long as this book survives either on some musty old bookcase shelf in the centuries to come or in a jillionth popular edition perhaps taught in a space-age music appreciation course, Freddy's memory and the memory of this book will be linked in the years to come.

Freddy Carr deserves to be in this book because wherever he is nowadays he's left us this album which is more entertaining than most cranked out by 1960's Nashville. According to the liner notes on the back of the album (which is more at least than we have to remember Don Lee by) for years Carr served as a back-up bandleader for certain "hit makers" not named.

This album evidently is part of his big push to get to the next level. Unless he had some sort of personal problem that we can't perceive without the benefit of seeing him in person I'd say he definitely deserved a larger audience. But, what the hell, maybe he was a boozer or maybe he had halitosis and no one had the heart to tell him. More likely he just didn't have the right agent or connections or perhaps he refused to kick back a chunk of his earnings to some scumbag music biz jackass. If you ever see a copy of this in a dollar bin somewhere, better pick it up.

Freddy delivers a spirited version of "Truck Drivin' Man," that is worth the space on your record shelf alone. He also sings two Hank Sr. tunes quite well: "Hey Good Lookin'" and "I Can't Help It." His band features a crackerjack steel guitar player and there are also some great acoustic guitar leads. The arrangements are ambitious as if Freddy and his band know this is their big shot. So many big names have walked through routine covers of "Oh Lonesome Me." Freddy on the other hand really delivers the goods.

The final song is a cover of another old chestnut scores of artists have covered "(I Washed My Hands In) Muddy Water" Freddy Carr's version isn't as gratuitously flashy or theatrical as many other readings and that's a good thing. I realized when listening to Freddy's version I had never in the past actually had a clue what the song was actually about.

I'd like to think that wherever Mr. Carr is today he's got a regular gig at a tavern he enjoys singing at and playing with his old buddies. If that's the case, in the long run he was probably lucky not to get sucked into some one-sided major label record deal. Wherever you are tonight Freddy Carr… I'm tipping my Lone Star to you.

HOWDY GLENN "I Can Almost See Houston" (1978) Indian Head Records. LP.

This is another one of those great obscure indie label albums. In the case of Howdy Glenn though, we're dealing with a fellow who did achieve a certain level of success. His name is listed in my record guide at least, which is more than you can say for most of the small label artists in this book. Howdy's singing skills are damn strong. He's obviously a real professional. His voice has that "charm" or "pizazz" or whatever you wanna call it that so many of the big boys on the charts during this time period had. I may be totally off base here, but I have to wonder if his skin color held him back. Yeah, sure, there's Charlie Pride and of course Ray Charles and a handful of others but the proportion of black country singers is simply way the hell low. It was never that there was a lack of blacks who dug country music. Chuck Berry and Ike Turner for instance both wrote in their autobiographies about being big fans of country music.

Back to Howdy Glenn, he sings eight songs out of ten, included on this album. Oddly, two instrumental tracks are included he wasn't involved in, one being a lame soprano sax led tune. Yuck. That can't be held against Howdy though. Chalk it up to the fact that small labels do bizarre things some times.

Side one has a couple fine drinking oriented songs. Check out "Has Been Honky-Tonk Queen." The only familiar cover song is the one that the liner notes state won a talent contest for Howdy and got his career off the ground "Old Dogs Children and Watermelon Wine" by Tom T. Hall.

I wish I had a stack of Howdy Glenn albums on my shelf, but it just wasn't to be so far as I know. I'd be glad to get an email someday from a fan of his telling me I'm wrong, that he sings at honky tonks several nights a week and is doing quite well.

The JACK WORTHINGTON SHOW (1973) NWI Records. LP.

According to the liner notes (written by an ex-boss at a trucking company) Jack Worthington got tired of his work hours interfering with his music making and drinking; so, he vowed to form a "knocked out musical TV record show thing." This album is a vinyl testament to his vision. He hired a couple buxom gal singers, a couple veteran middle-aged guys with a lot of arrangement skills and then he rounded out his eight-piece backing combo with a handful of 20-year-old guys wearing Edwardian suits with collars that are loud and bordering on obnoxious even by '70's standards.

A lot of this album stacks up with Dave Dudley and Del Reeves Jr. Efforts such as when Jack sings: "Truck Drivin' Man" "Little Ole Wine Drinker Me" and the "Wild Side of Life." Unfortunately, the backup band is allowed plenty of leeway creatively speaking, the album includes a wretched cover of a Loggins and Messina song and a couple game but only average sax solo tunes.

The tune that tips the scales in favor of this really being essential is a rip snorting version of the immortal Jerry Lee's "Great Balls of Fire" which doesn't top the killer, but rates very high among bar band versions. HHmmm. Upon further staring at the album cover and the bands suits I've concluded this is worth buying just for the cover. One of the band members is wearing a powder blue one that doesn't fit very well, as if he inherited it from another dude he replaced in the band.

JERRY LOWE "Don't Look Like Baby's Comin' Home" (1970's) LP.

What's that?? "Who the hell is Jerry Lowe?" Well, who the hell are you? This may be a rather obscure album outside of Mr. Lowe's native state of Indiana, but I can guarandamntee ya, if we were able to use one of those Star Trek gizmo's to transport Jerry Lowe and his band the Imperials, to modern day Austin to play in front of a Dale Watson audience the crowd would frigging flip. Hell, for that matter I bet Dale himself would.

Even though it could be a few years before we can transport great musical aggregations through time, at least we have this great album. On the cover Jerry sporting a huge set of mutton chop burns' is gazing at a picture of his main squeeze for whom (judging by the full ashtray and the instant coffee jar) he's been waiting up. This is a nice tie in with the title track of the album. Well done. It might have even looked better shot with color film, but what the hell. This album is a product of Imperial International Records, not Mercury or Columbia.

Side one continues with the excellent original: "House To a Home" and continues in a sort of tear in my beer vein with "Statue of a Fool." It's plain from the get go that Jerry's got a fine, fine voice and his band is pretty sharp. His steel player Pat Johnson especially stands out. Later on Jerry tackles some up tempo numbers including Merle Haggard's "Working Man Blues" and Buzz Rabin's round heeled gal saga "Call of the Wild."

This album is clearly better than most big label productions even given the fact that there was undoubtedly a small budget to work with. Damn, I hope somebody reading this will email me and tell me they own a couple subsequent Jerry Lowe albums. The Imperials and he would sound great tackling truck-driving songs I bet.

KEN LIGHTNER "Big Country" (1960's) (no record label!) LP.

Yep… that's right! You know you've got a real obscurity on your hands when there is no record label mentioned on the label or elsewhere. Judging by the fact that the pretty color landscape on the cover looks like New Mexico and this band is from Pennsylvania I think it's safe to say the cover is a generic shot provided by the pressing plant the band ordered these DIY records from. As stated before, I'm going out of my way whenever possible with this book to throw the spotlight onto obscure bands who are deserving.

Ken Lightner and his boys (The "Hayrider's") put together a nice enjoyable album here even if it is a bit low budget by comparison to Nashville productions. By the looks of the album overall and the lack of the usual hype within the back cover liner notes I'd say Ken had his sights set on selling these at appearances as opposed to using this as a stepping stone to one of the big record company's. There's nothing at all wrong with that.

Most of these tunes are originals including an absolute gem of a song "The Ole Coffee Hound" which I bet a lot of bigger artists would've loved to have covered. "Corner of Love" and "Big Big Love" are solid medium tempo optimistic romance numbers that remind me a bit of Carl Mann and Ricky Nelson. "Keep the Nickels" and "Wild Side of Town" are sordid tales of recent defeat in the game of love. The steel guitar player in this combo Al Foltin is really a fine musician.

This seems like a real "nice guy" band that probably played at the sort of places where folks wiped their boots before entering and nobody spit on the floor. I'm more partial personally to hell raising bands with attitude who sell oceans of beer. But, what the hell can you expect this far north of the Mason-Dixon line? Job well done.

NEAR BEER "Last Night" (1978) Cowboy Carl Records. LP.

You will never run out of fine country music albums to listen to as long as you are willing to do some legwork. I sure as hell am the first to admit that whereas I've heard loads of commercial records released by big labels, I haven't heard more than a sliver of the albums released by obscure artists on small regional labels. The music biz is a dirty, dirty racket in which for every singer who "succeeds" there's probably twenty sitting on back porches down in the boondocks who can perform just as well who never pursue a singing career.

The notion of singing and picking to achieve riches is a relatively new one. Even back in Greek and Roman times you can bet there were sodbusters sitting on their equivalent of back porches picking away for their own amusement and for their nearby neighbors to dance to.

This is where Illinois band: Near Beer comes in. I'm not sure if they ever went to Nashville to try to "make it" and frankly I don't care. What we have here is a group of a half dozen folks that played and sang outlaw country music in local midwestern taverns. For all I know, they're still at it... MORE POWER TO THEM.

Lead singer Wade Rivers doesn't have a very wide vocal range and probably can't croon like Conway, but he can sure as hell sell these songs. He sings on this album to a live audience of regular half drunk local's as opposed to a blank studio wall which creates a genuine spirit of F-U-N that can't be purchased or simulated in the best studios.

Waylon and Merle are covered here as you might expect: "Mama Tried" "This Time" "Lookin' for a Feelin' and "I Fought the law" is well handled and a couple originals are worked in. The album ends with a crackerjack "Redneck medley:" "London Homesick Blues/Up Against the Wall Redneck/Boney Fingers". There's a nice bunch of leads exchanged between electric guitar player Earl Sinks Jr. and accordion man Johnny Memphis.

A fine fifteen songer that never stalls out once. Another album you'll only find in a dollar bin that is easily worth $25 considering the enjoyment you'll get from it.

RALPH RAULERSON "Sings Country Gold" Music City Records. LP.

A fine, talented local '70's band from world famous Auburndale, Florida. This album is worthy thanks to the fact that the band performs absolute topnotch familiar material in ways we have never heard. Lots of cover bands are so by the numbers, they just lope along through songs almost unaware that they're bored too.

Ralph on the other hand really knows how to hit the sweet spots with his voice in the familiar songs. That's what separates "local bands" from "loser bands." The "Hank Medley" and "Oakie from Muskogee" are fine proof of this. The gospel tunes Tom T. Hall's "Me and Jesus" and Merle Haggard's "Jesus Take a Hold" are carried out just as well. Hell, the entire album is tasty as a bag of boiled peanuts, provided of course you can find one. I don't think many of these were pressed. Good luck.

RINK HARDIN "A Taste of Country & Western" ('60's) Time Records. LP.

What's that?? Who in the *@%! is Rink Hardin? Ironically the back cover liner notes declare that: "there have been numerous country artists who have fallen into obscurity. Rink Hardin is an artist who'll be around for a long time." Well, what the hell. I guess as they say hindsight is 20-20. The truth of the matter is that Rink Hardin deserves to be played on radio stations from coast to coast today as opposed to the awful, vile drivel spewing brackish manure coated-with-vomit smelling pop-crossover-country hogwash out of speakers nationwide like backed-up commodes from hell unleashing their fury.

Rink Hardin accomplishes more with this LP's first track "Wild and Wicked Life" than any of the jock-country hunks whose CD'S are being peddled down at Wal-Mart. You see, Rink Hardin sang and performed songs in the same vein as Hank Sr. and George Jones. This album is bloated with such tracks. To Rink Hardin a "crossover" was a way of turning around when you're driving on the freeway.

"Wild and Wicked Life" is a honky tonk number about a fella determined to drink beer in cold taverns until he erases his departed gal's memory. I suppose by today's standards the song would be unfit for airplay as it depicts the life of a possible "Substance Abuser". I suppose by today's standards a fellow should commit himself to "Anger Management" classes if he feels as potentially on edge and violent as the character in "When the Wine is Gone" yet another Rink classic that would be blackballed by Nashville today.

Steel guitar legend Pete Drake played on this Rink album. I suppose today his world class steel guitar talents would be considered "too hick" or "too twangy," or "too ____" (fill in the blanks) for him to be in demand by the Nashville corporate geniuses at all today.

Who is Rink Hardin? He's just one of the guys the likes of whom we should be hearing today on country radio on a regular basis. I fear he's probably running a putt-putt golf course somewhere these days. I hope I'm wrong; somebody locate Rink and tell me he's enjoying a long term engagement in some casino in the backwoods, somewhere where real country music is still demanded by the patrons.

SID LINARD "Juke Box Angel" (1976) Ovation Records. LP.

A thoroughly great country album from start to finish with well written all original songs including two catchy truck driving tunes. But, for some reason old Sid doesn't appear to have even been signed by one of the big labels. I can't find his name in any of my record guides, which means he had no chart success at all. How could this be?

I found this album the same way I find most of my records; combing around at thrift stores and flea markets. It's not that I'd enjoy his album better if he had been a big commercial success. Maybe he had his own reasons for not wanting to work full-time in the often-unsavory music biz. Maybe someday I'll find out the story behind him, then again maybe I won't. Ovation wasn't a flyspeck label. I'd say there's a good chance of other folks dredging up a copy of this since I'd guess 20-30,000 or so at the very least must've been pressed.

If you do find a copy, you'll undoubtedly appreciate Sid's fine voice and the great session players behind him including stalwarts Jerry Shook, Pete Drake and Hargus Robbins. My favorite track as usual is the drinking song "A Lord Calvert's Kind of Day". "The Undertaker's Gonna Have a Hardtime (Wiping the Smile off of my Face)" is a fine anthem for those of us dedicated to having fun in life.

On the morbid side is "The Easy Way Out" which deals with suicide. "I'm Not Gonna Let you Sock it to Me (Lying Down)" is a musical upraised finger towards the "ex". It'd sound great booming out of a tavern jukebox. Even though, many of even the very best country albums of all time can't claim to be without filler, this album is great from start to finish. There are no boring or sappy or tiresome songs whatsoever, which means you can plop back in your recliner with a six-pack and simply enjoy Sid's music without hopping up out of your seat every few minutes.

TERRY BRADSHAW "I'm so Lonesome I Could Cry" (1976) Mercury Records. LP.

The first time I spun this disc I expected it would be a big joke, an off key run through of hits that would still sell a reasonable number of copies based on Mr. Bradshaw's popularity as one of the greatest NFL quarterbacks of all time. Having seen Bradshaw work as a jovial Sunday grid iron color commentator for years at the very least I expected he'd be singing funny Jerry Reed or Ray Steven's type tunes. Damn, I was wrong.

Somebody really listened to Terry's voice (perhaps producer Jerry Kennedy) and evidently advised him to sing simply and not try to over deliver the songs. As a result, we have here a well-sung, low key collection of familiar classics. Terry covers two Hank Sr. songs (besides the title track "Take These Chains From My Heart") a Webb Pierce classic "Slowly" and an old chestnut, "Burning Bridges" to name a few. There are no up tempo songs or joke tunes with football references. If you weren't a football fan and didn't know any better and you happened to buy this album at your local K-Mart in 1976, you'd just nod along with the album.

This album is more than simply "not bad"… it's actually good.

Of course if I was sent to the studio with Pete Drake, Pig Robbins and the rest of the usual preferred '70's session dudes I might cut a decent album; they help quite a damned bit.

It's damned sure Terry can sing better than Jimmie the kid or Lefty Frizell or Johnny Cash could throw a football. Hell, he could damn sure deliver the goods on the football field better than bona fide athlete/singers Jim Reeves and Charlie Pride could on the baseball diamond.

9. OTHER COUNTRY'S COUNTRY

ELVIS COSTELLO "Almost Blue" (1981) Columbia Records. LP.

No, this isn't a joke album or a quirky experiment. It's a respectful country album that I imagine would only offend the super delicate sensitivities of that tiny percentage of traditionalist wacko's who are too stubborn to listen to anything but old 78's. Yunno; the kind of donkeys who still raise their eyebrows at CD's as being something evil. The production duties were handled by none other than the old master himself Billy Sherrill. What a break for Elvis. The result is an irresistible set of sweet vocal tracks. The way he croons "Sweet Dreams" is almost unbelievable. He gives ol' Patsy a run for her damn money as far as I'm concerned. I know that sounds impossible, but quaff down a six pack of Lone Star tall-boys while listening to this and I'm sure you might agree. Elvis rocks his way through a couple honky tonk classics in fine fashion "Tonight the Bottle Let Me Down" and "Why Don't you Love Me" but the arrangements aren't overly heavy handed. There's more piano pumping and steel guitar moaning going on than electric guitar twanging. He covers a couple tunes by his one time duet partner ("A Stranger in the House") George Jones: "Brown to Blue" and "Color of the Blues" the results are damn fine.

I'm going out on a limb here, this is definitely the best country music album ever performed by a singer born and raised in the U.K.

NEV NICHOLLS "Truckin' Around" (1975) RCA Australia. LP.

If you stop and think about it, it's only natural that Australia should have a Dave Dudley of it's own. Nev Nicholls doesn't merely ape Dudley, Sovine or Reeves or any other of our truck driving song potentates, but he's obviously been influenced by them just like so many other singers around the world. There's a few things about this album that set it apart from American albums.

First off the backing brass arrangements are right out of the 1960's Tijuana brass songbook. On the album cover there's ol' Nev standing in the parking lot of a truck stop down under; if you look closely the neon sign reads "Bimbo's Roadhouse" (OK.) "Time to Eat" (OK.) "Chinese Meals"... what the hell? I've never seen an American truck stop that advertised in neon that they served Chinese food. Chicken fried steak or omelets yeah. I guess they do things differently down under. Whereas Merle Haggard's "Movin' On" and Conway Twitty's "Hello Darlin'" borrow from yanks other songs like "Truckin' Around" "Havin' Fun at the

601" and especially, "The Great South State Truck Stop Disaster" are purely local in origin. Nicholls has a fine folksy voice and I can only wrap this up by expressing my wish that I had more than this one LP by Nev. I betcha' he's cut a slew of 'em.

"OUR KINDA COUNTRY" (early '60's) Columbia Records Australia. LP.

Proof that the #3 world wide country music nation is Australia. It figures, they have a frontier legacy complete with cowboys (they call 'em "stockmen") they have their own Jesse James (Ned Kelly) and their own truck stops and truck driving songs.

This 17 song collection is loaded with singers of different styles ranging from the veteran Aussie immortal drinking song King Slim Dusty ("A Pub With No Beer") to Rick and Thel Carey who contribute a thigh slapping domestic quarrel number "I'll Take the Dog". Buddy Williams "The Kelly Gang" is a ballsy ballad good to swing pints to whereas "Little Boy Lost" by Johnny Ashcroft makes me think of Roy Orbison tunes from this period.

"Why Don't You Try To Didgeridoo" by Alex Hood is easily as good as Rolf Harris's familiar (to Yanks) "Tie Me Kangaroo Down Sport." This album is a pleasure to listen to straight through. A couple of the folksier tunes aren't my cup of tea, but what the hell. This collection proves how strong a country music scene Australia has had for many, many years.

RINGO STARR "Beaucoups of Blues" (1971) Apple Records. LP.

What's that you say? How in the hell could former Beatle Ringo Starr pull off a quality country music LP? Gaze at the faces in the back cover band photo. Flanking Ringo is steel guitar legend Pete Drake and immortal drummer D.J. Fontana. Charlie Daniels sat in with his fiddle and Charlie McCoy, Jerry Reed and the Jordanaires were all in on the project too. Friends, Mom's Mabley could've cut a decent album with that kind of backing!

Several of the songs are really good including the title track, "$15 Draw" and drinking anthems "Wine Women and Loud Happy Song" and "Loser's Lounge". A few of the tunes start to drag a bit but as I've pointed out repeatedly only the very best albums can claim to be without filler. Ringo's vocals are very professional throughout. In the 1960's when John and Paul chose him to sing "Act Naturally" he surprised a lot of people by pulling off Buck's song damn well.

His friendly singing voice is blessed with a natural charisma. I'm not much of a Beatle fan at all. If I had to pick one of 'em to go fishing with it'd definitely be Ringo. If I had to pick an album from the mostly mediocre stack recorded by the solo ex-cuddly mop tops to play over and over on a desert Island it'd sure as hell be this one too.

STOMPIN' TOM CONNORS "To It and At It" Boot Records. LP

I just checked my most thorough record collector price guide. Checking under "Connors" we have Bob Connors,

Carol Connors, the "Rifleman" Chuck Connors, Greg, Norman and Seth Connors, but there isn't a single listing for Stompin' Tom Connors. Why? I figger it's because he's a proud super patriot Canadian and he doesn't want to kiss the necessary asses to gain fame in the U.S.

Stompin' Tom is as Canadian a singer as I've ever heard. His accent is quite similar to that of his fellow countryman Hank Snow whom I'm unsure whether he regards as an influence or as a stooge for selling out to us yanks. All kidding aside, I admire Connor's chest thumping Canadian pride. This album may send you running to those hitherto never used pages in the back of your atlas in the middle of the first song since geographical references fly by fast and furious. "Prince Edward Island Happy Birthday" "New Brunswick and Mary" and the catchy "Manitoba" are all well written proud patriotic numbers showing Tom at his best.

"To It and At It" is a fun tongue twister that chastises lay about slackers. "Golden Gone Bye" is an old school traditional sounding classic that proves to me that Tom could've succeeded quite well in Nashville if he had wanted to; I'm glad he didn't. I love his feisty, distinctive style. I spotted a guy at a record show in NYC who was wearing a "Stompin' Tom" T-shirt; I complimented the fellow and asked him if the legend ever came down to the States to play. He turned red and looked away not wanting to embarrass me by pointing out how stupid my question was to a fan of Stompin' Tom's. It was as if I had asked if Ozzy Osbourne wanted to play at a Sunday school picnic in Salt Lake City, or if Stevie Wonder looked forward to being booked at a Klan rally.

TOM JONES "Green Green Grass of Home" Decca Records Australia. LP.

What's that you say? is ol' hip swinging, Las Vegas panties magnet Tom Jones "country"? Of course. His roots lead back to a tiny village in Wales--not London. His daddy was a lifelong coal miner and his musical idol as a youth was our own Dixie fried piano protégé Jerry Lee Lewis. A sparse few of these tunes are a bit "pop" to be considered country on their own merits, but you could say that about a lot of American bumpkins including Conway and Dolly.

For the most part Tom tackles material that would be at home in many albums included in this book including, "Ring of Fire" "Sixteen Tons" (his daddy must've been proud to hear that one) "Detroit City" and of course the title song. My favorite from this batch is "He'll Have to go" in which Tom seems to be busting his tail to pay loving tribute to a great crooner he grew up listening to: Jim Reeves. Tom's band does an XLNT and appropriate job here. Lots of twangy string-bending guitar and vocal accompaniments that would likely make Anita Kerr nod her head in approval.

10. ALL THE OUTLAWS

ALVIN CROW "High Riding" (1977) Polydor. LP.

This album is a nifty showcase of the talents of Alvin Crow and his band the Pleasant Valley Boys. It demonstrates the praiseworthy lingering influence of Western Swing upon baby boomer generation musicos in Texas. Don't get me wrong; there's nary a smidgeon of hippie contamination to be found in these grooves. When it comes to '70's country albums recorded by folks from this age group, more often than it's as unpleasant to my ears as a galling load of Poco or Canned Heat crud.

There's definitely a rowdy edge to this album. The song "(The Texas Kid's) Retirement Run" is unabashedly about smuggling weed. That wouldn't have shocked the outlaw country fan base in Austin at the time, but the local Tom Landry worshipping squares would have been mortified if they caught wind of it. The saxophone lead parts seem to suffer at times from a case of '70's bar band aesthetic taint. Other than that I'm sure Bob Wills would approve. I really admire the tribute song to him: "Turkey Texas (Home of Bob Wills)." The broad range of tunes from the rambunctious "Wine Me Up" to the soft spoken salute to a legendary Austin honky tonk) "The Broken Spoke Waltz" is definitely worth hoisting your beer stein (or bong) to. As of the time of this writing you can still see Alvin Crow performing live down here in the Austin, Texas area on a frequent basis. Viva Alvin Crow.

BUZZ RABIN "Cross Country Cowboy" (1974) Elektra Records. LP.

A debut album by a helluva songwriter you can file with your most frequently played outlaw country LPs. The album begins and ends with pleasing versions of the title track which is a bittersweet apocalyptic lament of sorts. Sandwiched in between is the title track from Ringo Starr's country album, "Beaucoups of Blues" the sad "Death of a Derelict" and "The Drifter" which sounds to me like a tip of the fifth to Hank Sr. Production duties on this album were handled by legendary Steel King Pete Drake.

I'm not sure who's idea it was to include 30-40 second bluegrass passages between tracks, but I like it. It kinda helps to clear my head like a booze shot between beers. Rabin gets extra points for posing in jolly fashion on the cover with a glass of whiskey and one of those tipped cigars so popular in the 1970's. Willie and Waylon fans should dig this up at all costs.

DAVID ALLAN COE "The Best of" (1984) CBS/Pair Records. 2-LP.

Of course there are plenty of "best of" collections of D.A.C. material to choose from. This two vinyl LP, sixteen song anthology is hands down the best I've seen and the one that most often sits in a place of honor amongst the little pile of LPs, right by my turntable that rarely gets filed away onto a shelf.

Side one starts off with, "Desperado's Waiting For the Train." David's version is the best ever recorded and it's topped off with a dramatic fiddle part that never fails to chill me. The "perfect" country music song "You Never Even Called Me By My Name" is a highlight along with Coe's version of "... Shove It" (not quite as good as Paycheck's, but still worth stomping around yer living room floor over).

The songs range from a wild saga of Coe's reform school years, "Merle And Me" to a somber version of his composition Tanya Tucker sold way better on: "Would You Lay With Me (In a Field of Stone)". A must have album already and we haven't even gotten to "Longhaired Redneck," "Waylon Willie and Me" and a playful "male" send up of "Stand By Your Man."

I don't recommend that any fans of D.A.C. get in a rut by only listening to his best known songs. You really do have to go out eventually and find a dozen or so albums to stand any chance at discovering what he's all about. This collection (good luck finding it!) is simply the best I've seen of his better known mandatory songs.

DAVID ALLAN COE "Rides Again" (1977) Columbia Records LP.

Definitely D.A.C. during one of his best phases, that of "The Mysterious Rhinestone Cowboy" yeah, yeah it can take a few listens for fans unfamiliar with David to figure out what the hell he's all about, but that's part of the fun. Side one begins and ends with the classic hit: "Waylon, Willie and Me" a beautiful, rebellious and invigorating song. Next thing you know David has switched gears entirely and is singing about his four wives in: "The House We've Been Calling Home." You may ask: "isn't that illegal?" or "is he serious?" Friend, that's just D.A.C. toying with your mind. Relax and enjoy the ride.

"Young Dallas Cowboy" and "A Sense of Humor" sound like David's gettin' pissed off. Side two's, "Lately I've Been Thinking Too Much Lately" may hold the key. The closing number, "If That Ain't Country" stands out as an all time country classic about "poor white trash" and poverty on a par with the best work of even Johnny Cash, who David name drops during the chorus. The first several times I heard it as a new Coe acolyte I suspected he was trying to establish his credibility through Johnny's name, but the more I listen to it the more convinced I am that in a roundabout way he's gloating because he knows that this song is so strong for once he's topped Cash at his own game. David Allan Coe is that good once in a while.

You don't know what you're gonna see when you see D.A.C. perform live; he might sing slow relationship ballads or veer off into an X-rated number. He might stop the show to perform magic tricks or call Kid Rock up on stage. Pro wrestler Roddy Piper once said in a TV interview: "just when you think you have all the answers… I change the questions." That applies to D.A.C. perfectly. So, my advice to you is quit trying to figure him out and enjoy his music and you'll be best off.

JOHNNY PAYCHECK "The Real Mr. Heartache" (1996) CD.

I really love the handful of Paycheck hits such as "Satin Sheets" "... Shove It" and others you occasionally hear on classic country radio stations. The fact is though, Johnny's more obscure 60's recordings for the "Lil' Darlin'" label are considered the real deal by a lot of serious country fans in the same way lots of Elvis fans prefer the King's rarely heard pre-RCA Sun label songs.

When I first heard this CD as a new release at the Tower Records store I worked at in 1996 I was amazed. I had been listening to the same Epic label recordings by Paycheck for years like everybody else. It's not unusual to discover three or four forgotten small label gems by a recording artist. This disc though, is loaded with 24 tracks as damn potent as anything else Johnny ever recorded. When you add Paycheck's mountain of stellar "lost" Lil' Darlin' recordings to the list of his later tip top big label hits it becomes apparent that he has to be considered amongst the absolute greatest country singers ever.

It seemed strange at first listen that these 24 catchy songs (and many others recorded during the same period not included here) received such little fanfare when they were first issued between 1964-1968. When you think about it though and listen to the lyrics a few more times, these songs were too hardcore, simply way ahead of their time in the happy face '60's. These aren't merely sad tales of love gone wrong; these are songs about going plumb haywire (such as in, "I'm Barely Hangin' On To Me" and "The Late and Great Me") getting obliterated on alcohol nightly ala Hank Sr., George and so many others, "Motel Time Again" and in the case of one song "Pardon Me I've Got Someone To Kill." The song ends in a double murder/suicide. It's hard to imagine songs like these blending back to back on the radio with Glen Campbell style pop crossover fluff in the '60's!

These songs are simply brutally honest and realistic. Paycheck's vocals are sarcastic at times; "It's a Mighty Thin Line Between Love and Hate" and "If I'm Gonna Sink I Might As Well Go to the Bottom" and icy and detached when appropriate, "My Baby Don't Love Me Anymore." The amazing "(Like me) You'll Recover in Time" is a song in which Johnny's character encounters an ex-lover who drove him over the edge, now a fellow patient at a mental institution.

The well-chosen, sometimes eerie musical arrangements work really well to convey the desperate and sometimes psychotic nature of the songs. Band session leader Lloyd Green does an especially swell job weaving in and out of the picture in a creepy manner with his steel guitar. The band perfectly compliments Paycheck's often-desperate voice.

What more can we ask for from a collection of country songs? The late Johnny Paycheck never received his due recognition in his lifetime as one of the ultimate handful of country music grandmasters. This book will do what it can to rectify the situation.

Johnny Paycheck "Armed & Crazy" (1978) Epic. LP.

If you look under "outlaw country" in any one of the many country music encyclopedias published over the last 30 years you will see a picture of either Waylon and Willie, both of them or the record breaking outlaw compilation LP Waylon organized that became the biggest selling (at that time) country LP ever.

As mighty as Mr. and Mrs. Waylon's and Willie and Tompall's talents were during that time period it's plain in retrospect that two men "out outlawed" the better known outlaws: Johnny Paycheck and David Allen Coe. Both fella's did a lot of time behind bars over the years and their song material has often reflected the hard lives they've led. Out of 70 plus years of country singers popping pills like candy, guzzling whiskey by the gallon and making like rabbits with honky tonk cuties I'll hereby nominate D.A.C. and Paycheck as the supreme outlaws of the entire country music tradition. Not because they may have popped more or snorted more or screwed more or drank more, but because their music has reflected their wild wicked ways so well.

"Armed and Crazy" goes miles beyond merely challenging the record companies authority in a good natured manner. The dangerous statements made on this LP are a far cry past subtle pot smoking references. Paycheck challenges the most serious branch of our government with "Me and the I.R.S.."

Holy shit! The title song opens with a blistering rock riff that leads into a frantic tale about robbing a grocery store "Disguised As a Little Old Lady." "Thanks to the Cat House I'm in the Dog House with You" is an unrepentant jolly tune about the results of a trip to the local brothel. "Mainline" isn't a typical discreet cheatin' song, it's written from the point of view of an absolute human weasel boasting and gloating over how little money or commitment he has to make to his relationship compared to the "Mainline" whose wife he's diddling. And then there's the album ending "Outlaws Prayer" which is a spoken word retort to holier than thou church folk. Johnny's reading of it is flawless and moving. All in all, this album seems as feisty and pissed off as the punk rock bands who were also having a banner year in 1978.

JOHNNY PAYCHECK "At Carnegie Hall" (1966) Little Darlin'. LP.

No Virginia, this album wasn't recorded at Carnegie Hall. It's a studio representation of songs from his set list when he played there. I believe this is Paycheck's first of so many great full length LPs to come. Each side starts with a popular classic as if the strategy is to lure new listeners: "King of the Road" and "Ballad of the Green Berets." Both tunes are covered fine enough, but the real table thumping gems are the original numbers.

The gritty "Bayou Bum" not only follows "King of the Road" it chews it up and spits it out. It's a helluva better song. "He's In a Hurry (To Get Home to My Wife)" in which Johnny sings the part of a jealous fellow who got dumped for screwing up just once, is deadpanned perfectly. The prison break tune, "Ballad of Frisco Bay" is morbid and ugly. I love it. "Big Town Baby" is topnotch honky tonk work and proof to me Johnny had nothing to do with the "aw shucks" liner notes Aubrey Mayhew undoubtedly wrote and signed his name to.

For a first LP the lines are sung in such a seasoned, cool manner. This is proof Paycheck was great from the very start. This album even stacks up to his former boss George Jones LPs from this same period.

JOHNNY PAYCHECK "Bars-Booze-Blondes" Little Darlin' LP.

The album title is well chosen and doesn't beat around the bush. These brilliant songs are almost all from the great Paycheck and Mayhew partnership. Johnny may have had greater temporary commercial success later in his career but it's his Little Darlin' label material that will stand for the ages with the best honky tonk music ever recorded.

These songs examine in frightening depth the lustful, despondent and often desperate, denizens of local bars across the USA. This album is more American than apple pie. "The Pint of no Return" "We're the Kind of People" and "I Drop More Than I Drink" are masterpieces of interpretation of the unmitigated human condition; in other words they show just how low people can go.

"Two Candles One Dinner and a Bottle" is a thoughtful variation from the main theme. It's written from the perspective of a would-be cheater whose conscience sends him home at the last minute. "Meanest Jukebox in Town" and "Haven for Angel's Unaware" are both chock full of bar room wisdom that egghead sociologists can look back to a hundred years from now for a realistic look at what went on in the tavern's and lounges of the late 20th century.

JOHNNY PAYCHECK "Jukebox Charlie" 'Lil Darlin'. LP

This album is jam packed with songs so potent they must've made a lot of listeners used to innocuous George Morgan type ballads cringe. The musicians used include the amazing Lloyd Green whose steel guitar is the perfect axe to compliment Johnny's bitter and sometimes spine tingling vocals. Yeah, yeah, a lot of honky tonk singers can deliver an adultery song that brings folks almost to tears; Johnny Paycheck goes beyond most of them and scares the shit out of 'em. These are songs steeped in the realistic miseries of chronic alcoholism. Twenty years before Johnny's old employer and drinking pal George Jones sang about "Still Doing Time" Johnny with Aubrey Mayhew's assistance was cranking out entire albums like this one that are right up there with ol' Possum's best work.

"Down at Kelley's" is a classic tale of marital malfunction. When I hear "Motel Time Again" I think of Johnny in real life staggering around confused trying to figure out where to sleep it off. This version of "Apartment #9" is clearly more heartfelt than any other I've ever heard. The only song that's off kilter is the strange album closer "Malinche" which seems to be about the explorer Cortez? What? Oh well.. 13 out of 14 ain't bad. I usually consume enough beers and shots when I'm listening to Paycheck the last song could've been about "Barney."

JOHNNY PAYCHECK "New York Town" (1980) Epic. LP.

Just for the record, in spite of what Buck Owen's anti-Big Apple, song may have you thinking, NYC has a damned enthusiastic country music audience. Now, fanny kickin' live outlaw country albums require foot stompin' audiences ready to help the band light the commodes ablaze. Enjoying the success of his "..Shove It" phase, Paycheck could've recorded his live album anywhere, but he chose the Lone Star Cafe in NYC (take that Buck). The result is a frenzied set that must've left the anything but jaded big city folks swinging from the nearest neon Hamms sign. This is one of the best live albums I've heard from any genre of music. It's not just a token run through of hits, you could find yourself playing this album instead of Paycheck's always top notch studio albums. The last eighty percent of side two consists of a live run of songs I've queued up over and over and over again both for house-guests and for my own personal enjoyment while getting tanked up in the middle of the night. It begins with: "11 Months and 29 Days" which includes a blistering wailing tenor sax solo by Big Murph, one of Paycheck's top hands. Without let up the band rolls into "Stay Away From the Cocaine Train" and right into the notorious anthem, "Me and the I.R.S." The closer is of course "Take This Job and Shove It" played and sung rowdy as hell.

Side one ain't half bad either, but that final run of songs on side two is amazing. I'd pay a pretty penny to see a video of this show. I'd French kiss a pit bull's bung-hole. I'd quit drinking for a week… er, well... let's not be hasty. I gotta draw the line somewhere, but you get the idea.

MOE BANDY "Greatest Hits" (1982) Columbia Records. LP.

There's something I don't understand about this album. The liner notes are written by Moe, fine enough, but they're written from the standpoint of a man at the end of his career. Hell, in 1982 Moe was just hitting his stride. If what happened to Nashville hadn't happened we'd be seeing him to this day on TV at annual award shows filling the shoes of the legendary guys who are getting older and are in relatively poor health. By now he would've racked up a helluva pile of great songs.

But no, instead of Moe, we've been force fed for years by Nashville a steady stream of handsome, less talented "studs" with mediocre samey-sounding voices. Oh yeah, these hunks talk occasionally about being fans of Hank Sr. and George Jones, but they're just running their mouths. They're nothing but a bunch of James Taylor and Loggins and Messina fans sporting cowboy hats.

One of Moe's specialties is cheating songs of course and this album is chock of great ones: "It Was Always So Easy (To Find An Unhappy Woman)" "It's a Cheating Situation," and "I Cheated Me Right Out of You." My personal favorite is "Hank Williams You Wrote My Life."

Last I heard Moe Bandy has been up in Branson singing. I hope he's happy and I'm glad he's still at it, but what a waste of talent!

MOE BANDY "Here I am Drunk Again" (1976) Columbia Records. LP.

The cover of this record is worth the price of the album alone. Thanks to the creativity of Columbia Record's art department we are treated to a vision of the average beer drinkers ultimate fantasy. Moe is seen totally submerged in the bottom of a full beer mug. When you see a cover like this it's a good bet you're in for a fine batch of drinking and cheatin' songs and not just a double handful of boring relationship songs.

This album was released a couple years on into Moe's career. He eventually racked up a respectable number of hits and established himself as thee great young honky tonk singer to emerge in the '70's. Unfortunately it seems like Moe's career sure as hell wasn't helped by the upheaval in Nashville in the 1980's. I guess the geniuses in Music City thought his ass didn't look inviting enough in a pair of tight jeans to risk keeping around (for that matter I bet even ol' Hank's boney old butt wouldn't have either).

This album isn't an exploitation piece with delirious images of green snakes or tales of neglected half starved children. It's got the sort of songs ordinary schlubs who work at tire stores can relate to such as: "If I Had Someone to Cheat On" which is a nice twist on a time worn theme. "Please Take Her Home" is a sad sort of pre-cheating number meant to nip the affair in the bud before it turns into a grisly Paycheck type post coitus revenge ditty.

The title song "Here I Am Drunk Again" isn't a lusty, jolly drinking tune. It's a bit sad like a lot of the songs on this album. It's appeal is for jilted guys who wind up holding down a stool more or less against their will, and the ladies who've dumped them.

Moe closes out a fine set with "The Man That You Once Knew" a sad farewell that politely asks the eternal question: "see what you've done to me bitch?"

"REDNECKS WHITE SOCKS & BLUE RIBBON BEER" (1980) RCA/Tee Vee Records. Compilation LP.

There have been thousands of country music compilation LPs released over the years. Most of them are either

Christmas collections or label "samplers" to familiarize fans with its stable of artists. The problem I have with label compilations is that most of them include a goodly dose of forgettable, bland love ballads. The great exception to the rule is truck driving song compilations which are almost one hundred percent worth owning. This album is one of the most amazing and unique comp's you'll ever see because it follows a theme that always guarantees a damn good top notch listen; it's a collection of twenty drinking songs!

If I were turned loose with a pass key to the RCA Record vaults in Nashville and asked to assemble a late '70's collection of boozin' tunes that pleased me yet still offered a possibility to sell worth a damn via TV ads, I'd very likely come up with something like this.

The first two songs right out of the gate are holy: "Redneck" (The Redneck National Anthem) by Vernon Oxford and, "Rednecks, White Socks and Blue Ribbon Beer" by Johnny Russell. Next we have "She's Acting Single (I'm Drinking Doubles)" by the great Gary Stewart who is also represented on this album by "Whiskey Trip" and "Drinkin' Thing." Other highlights are "Pop a Top" by Jim Ed Brown, "Dropkick Me Jesus", "The Winner" by Bobby Bare, Jerry Reed's hilarious "I'm Just a Redneck in a Rock 'n Roll Bar" and the goofy exploitation "Sheriff of Boone County" by Kenny Price.

Not one sappy romance number can be found on this disc. That's saying something. Go check your own collection of country compilations and you'll see what I mean. This album is like a tape you'd make ahead of time for a party or perhaps a cassette batch of songs for a like minded lush pal whose wife tossed him out and kept the stereo and records.

WANTED: THE OUTLAWS (1977) RCA Records. Compilation. LP.

This album held the distinction for several years as the biggest selling country music album of all time. Does it live up to it's reputation? Hell yeah. Are these folks the wildest outlaws in the annals of C&W history? Hell no. So what? A handful of the greatest country songs from the '70's are found within.

Side one is devoted to Waylon Jennings and Jessi Colter (OK, she probably got her spot on this album due to the fact she's Mrs. Jennings. She was one of the great all time musician wives though for putting up with his shit. I love her for that). Waylon's tunes: "My Heroes Have Always Been Cowboys" and "Honky Tonk Heroes" are certifiably great. Jesse follows up with a couple tunes that prove she's wasting her time in the Jennings kitchen.

Side two, Waylon and Willie tag team on "Good Hearted Woman" which is a total empty chucking goddamned smash of course. One of Willie's best ever songs, "Me And Paul," is included. It's a sort of ballad about Willie and his drummer's hit parade of substance abuse over the years. Next Willie almost steals the show with a truly immortal tune: Yesterday's Wine" but at the last minute Tompall Glaser romps off with the bragging rights with a cool cover of Jimmie Rodger's "T for Texas" and perhaps his career moment a badass rendition one of Shel Silverstein's best ever songs: "Put Another Log on the Fire." If you're keeping score, that's a pretty damned high ratio of songs still being played on classic country radio and covered in bars by singers everywhere.

WAYLON JENNINGS s/t Vocalion Records. LP

As of this writing, if you visit the official Gram Parsons homepage on the internet your eyes will be treated to the often stated claim that the late Mr. Parsons was "The World's First and Most Outrageous Country Rock musician." The notion that Parsons invented country-rock is rarely challenged; yet it's an asinine falsehood that probably dates back to the halcyon days when millionaire's son Gram did drugs with all the right rock opinion leaders in the '70's.

Brother, you'd have to be high on dope to screw up the basic mathematics involved. Between 1963-1965 Parsons was performing Kingston Trio style folk music with a band called the Shiloh's. It didn't rock... it wasn't country. Waylon was one of Buddy Holly's Crickets. Buddy took Waylon to the studio and produced his very first recording session.

His advice to budding young rocker Waylon was that he had a country oriented voice. Waylon was on the scene the "day the music died." After a period of mourning he embarked on a solo career utilizing Buddy's advice. By 1964 he had produced the songs on this LP for various labels. Included here is a jangly 1964 version of Dylan's "Don't Think Twice It's All Right" that pre-dates the Byrds by a long shot.

Waylon sings a rousing rocking version of "White Lightnin'" which was penned by the, "Big Bopper," who died alongside Buddy. The rest of the songs include a great version of Buck Owen's "Loves Gonna Live Here Again" and a cover of Cajun-hick tune "Big Mamou." Rock and Roll icon (and another Jennings pal) Roy Orbison's "Crying" is also covered here with pretty damn fine results.

The songs included on this LP are only a few of many recorded by Waylon by 1964. All down the line he's got one foot in country and the other rooted in rock and roll. Yet Gram Parsons is hailed as the original country-rock artist? What an obvious crock of shit! I'm actually disappointed that it takes a guy like me to point out the fact that you'll read this blatant lie in virtually every country music "encyclopedia" in print.

This is proof that to the mindless masses of the "classic rock era" with their dope-addled brains anything read in Rolling Stone magazine is simply considered from that day forth the holy truth. It's a bit more surprising how many "alternative" country types can be found regurgitating the Parsons myth; Then again, let's not give these folks too much credit. These are the same brainiac's who consider the late Grams former gal-pal Emmylou Harris some sort of traditional country touchstone. Hah! Don't get me started again.

WAYLON JENNINGS "Greatest Hits" (1979) RCA Records LP.

Country music singers tend to sound like other country singers. That's not meant to be a put down. Vocalists from every other genre tend to sound alike especially to the casual listener. Tony Bennett and Andy Williams and a lot of the other crooners from "music of your life" type radio stations sound a lot alike to me and so do rappers and reggae singers. The more music you listen to closely from any style of music the more trained your ear is to differentiate between different stylists. After listening to such a wide variety of country singers in the process of researching this book I learned quite a bit about the evolution of certain styles. Merle Haggard's voice sounds to me a bit like Buck Owens on his duets album with Bonnie Owens. He sounds like Lefty at other times, although of course most of the time as the years went by Merle just sounded like Merle. Not surprisingly, scads of singers from the ranks of bar bands in turn sound a lot like ol' Hag at times.

After listening to several hundred albums in the process of writing this book I can now actually hear Jimmie Rodgers influence in some of Hank Snow's work and I can also pinpoint songs of his which sound like they likely influenced Willie Nelson. There are times when I'm driving down the road listening to a classic country station when I'm not sure whether I'm listening to Mickey Gilley, his cousin Jerry Lee Lewis or Charlie Rich.

There are of course a few unique singers who don't sound all that much like anybody else. Waylon Jennings was one of those. When one of his songs is played on the radio you often don't even need to hear Waylon's voice to know it's his song. He was one of a tiny handful of musicians from all the different forms of popular music who actually had his own trademark rhythm. His voice separated him from the pack even more though. It was macho and deep and manly when necessary, yet tender "for the ladies" too at times.

This album includes several irresistibly good familiar songs from his long recording career: "Only Daddy That'll Walk the Line" "Are You Sure Hank Done it This Way" "Ladies Love Outlaws" and "Good Hearted Woman."

About the only complaint I have about this album is it's too short. You can't possibly expect to cover Waylon's career on one vinyl LP. You definitely need to seek out a variety of albums to have all of his songs you need.

WAYLON JENNINGS "I've Always Been Crazy" (1978) RCA Records. LP.

An inspired masterpiece that really stands out amongst Waylon's huge legacy of fine albums many of which (through no fault of Waylon's) recycle the same songs over and over. It leads off with "I've Always Been Crazy" which is a self effacing Bukowski-ish lyric that proves what a tremendous grasp on things Waylon had as opposed to the wimpy California country rock trendies.

He follows up with "Don't You Think This Outlaw Bits Done Gone out of Hand" which brings right out front a major drug bust he was involved in. Side two begins with a bit of unfinished business that I'd like to think Waylon has been saving for this moment in his career when he had such a huge audience; he sings a Buddy Holly medley which pays tribute to his old pal whose fame has perhaps dipped a bit in the jaded late '70's. Talk about a loving tribue. Next he tips his hat to his old roomie Johnny with a version of, "I Walk the Line" and then he salutes Merle with "Tonight the Bottle Let Me Down." What gives?? Did Waylon think he was going to prison for the drug bust? Is this meant to be some sort of farewell album in case of the worst case scenario?

Either way it's a bloody good piece of work even by his standards at the very least. This is his most crucial album in my humble opinion right after his various hits collections.

WILLIE NELSON /WEBB PIERCE "In the Jailhouse Now" (1982) Columbia Records. LP.

It seems to me that Willie Nelson has really put a lot of effort into the albums he recorded with other folks. His work with Leon Russell and this album with the late great Webb Pierce are two fine examples.

The cover photos are the sort that I keep studying over and over. Lets face it, this is a musical meeting of two of country music's outsiders, troublemakers to some degree in the eyes of the Nashville establishment. As legendarily laid back as Willie is, you can tell by looking at his expression he wasn't about to screw up in front of a boyhood hero of this magnitude. Webb, who was getting up there in years by 1982 appears to be relaxed on the cover probably content in knowing it's Willies band set to back them up, so let Willie do the worrying and stressing. Willie's decked out not in his sneakers and tank top as usual but rather in a beautiful Marlboro Man fringed leather jacket and a really nice pair of boots and a pearl gray cowboy hat instead of a mere rolled up bandana.

Willie certainly put his best foot forward here working out tight arrangements with his band. There's no sign of excessive backup vocals, lavish strings or loosely played folk-rock on this album. It's just an all business, fat sounding honky tonk ensemble.

This album is action packed with several of my all time Webb Pierce favorites. It starts off with: "There Stands the Glass" "Wondering" and the title track Jimmie Rodger's tune "In the Jailhouse Now". These three songs alone accompanied by seven silent tracks would still top 99% of country albums ever recorded. Webb and Willie both sing warmly and masterfully. This is on the opposite end of the spectrum from Moe Bandy and Joe Stampley and their wacky barroom buddy schtick.

"Slowly" "Backstreet Affair" "More and More" etc. The performances seem intense rather than loose run throughs. A relatively unpredictable selection, "Heebie Jeebie Blues" which ends side one deserves special mention.

WILLIE NELSON & LEON RUSSELL "One For the Road" (1979) Columbia Records. 2 LP set.

Disc one is a rundown of a slew of great old dusty standards sung by Willie and Leon backed by Willie's band at their best. "Don't Fence Me In" "Sioux City Sue" and the old Governor Jimmy Davis tune, "You Are My Sunshine" all really tickle my fancy. The arrangements are sparse but very, very pretty. I played this at a get together in my basement once for some guests and I'll be damned if it didn't steal the spotlight away from all the louder, more aggressive stuff I had also played that night. Hank and Elvis are covered back to back: "I Saw the Light" and "Heartbreak Hotel."

Disc two finds Willie singing with Leon providing the music with a variety of keyboards ranging from a traditional piano to smokey, synth-strings. "Summertime" "Am I Blue" "Stormy Weather" and other tunes Grandma really dug way back when are crooned with a great deal of charisma and personality. This album really clicks. Maybe it's because these guys rarely get to play the good old time shit they heard when they were young, beardless and impressionable.

WILLIE NELSON: "Willie and Family Live" Columbia Records. 2 LP set.

I scoffed at Willie at the time this was released. I couldn't deal with his voice. As the years went by and I got deeper and deeper into country music I kept coming back again and again to listen to him with fresh ears every couple years or so. The reason I kept trying was the obvious fact that he's such an incredible song writer. Finally one day my buddy Jeff Clayton (who had once had the same "problem" with Willie's voice) came out and admitted that he had seen the light at one of his live shows.

He asked me to take his word for it and try to hear Willie live so that I could come over to the right side of the fence. Hallelujah! I found a copy of this album and finally figured out where Mr. Nelson is coming from. I'm now able to listen with pleasure to quite a few of his albums. This one is the absolute best in my opinion. It's two albums worth of his best material ranging from the tune Patsy Cline made so famous "Crazy" and the immortal "Nightlife" with it's boozy words and distinctive chords, to a fine medley from the "Red Headed Strange" album that many declare is his best.

After a break and a change of platters, Willie and family romp out a hit parade of outlaw classics like "I Gotta Get Drunk" "Whiskey River" and "The Only Daddy That'll Walk the Line." Cousin Johnny Paycheck even comes out to sing "... Shove It." I've skimmed over a lot of great material such as; "Good Hearted Woman" "If You've Got the Money I've Got the Time" and "Bloody Mary Morning." There are no weak spots; Willie never talks sappy to the audience even though this was recorded in Las Vegas in the '70's. Just two great platters that can and should be played back to back. If you haven't come around to understanding and appreciating Willie Nelson I recommend this remedy.

11. PIONEERS

"BOB WILLS & His TEXAS PLAYBOYS "Ultimate Collection" CD.

As the great Mr. Wills would say: "AAHH Hah!!!" Recording facilities were still rather sketchy when Mr. Wills and Co. trod the earth. That's not to say you shouldn't regularly play these twenty-six classic songs in your home, but you gotta find 'em first since they were issued as 78 rpm records. That little glitch makes this $5 CD from Israel a convenient and all around pleasurable item to have around. For those that need reminding, this is the man who blended traditional fiddle tune sounds with jazz, blues and early swing. This is the man who took a solemn oath never to play music people couldn't dance to. This is the man largely responsible for the entire sub genre known as Western

Swing, existing and thriving even today across America. Ask the folks from Asleep at the Wheel, Alvin Crow, or Merle Haggard. As the late great Waylon Jennings sang 30 years ago now: “Bob Wills Is Still the King.” Damn, he summed that up well. You’ve heard “San Antonio Rose” “Time Changes Everything” “Take Me Back to Tulsa” “Stay a Little Longer” sung and played by a jillion other artists.

For years and years Bob Wills and several versatile lineups performed these elegant numbers for crowds of folks in ballrooms, taprooms, grog shops and State fairs. This accumulated cream of the Will’s songbook is worth licking a toad to get. My personal faves are “Osage Stomp” and “Steel Guitar Rag.”

The BRISTOL SESSIONS (Country Music Foundation) 2 LP set.

The cover has a worthy quotation from the great Johnny Cash: "These recordings in Bristol in 1927 are the single most important event in the history of country music." Legendary talent scout Ralph Peer discovered both Jimmie Rodgers and the Carter family during the ten days that made up this infamous mobile recording unit talent search. It's worth the price of this double LP (loaded with detailed valuable liner notes within the gatefold sleeve) just to have the first recordings by those monumental acts.

They sure as hell weren't the only artists recorded by Peer that stand the test of time. Going into the session Ernest Stoneman who lived a couple towns down the road from the Carters was already an established star of sorts and veteran of a hundred or so recordings for a few different record companies. He used his family to back him which means the

Stonemans technically preceded the Carters as a family country dynasty.

It seems to me the two families sound more alike than surf vocal groups the Beach Boys and Jan and Dean. The Stonemans dark gospel/moral passion play tunes "Midnight on the Stormy Deep" and "The Resurrection" are just barely edged by the Carters "The Wandering Boy" and "The Storms Are on the Ocean" thanks to their stronger solo voices and thanks to the fact that Maybelle Carter (Johnny Cash's mother-in-law) picked guitar in a manner unequaled by any other player at these sessions.

Jimmie Rodgers "Sleep Baby Sleep" and "The Soldiers Sweetheart" are great tunes, but they are matched easily by train death song King blind Alfred Reed who chips in with "The Wreck of the Virginian." Several others hang in there equally well. Modern day listeners might think they're listening to Boone county's finest Hazil Adkins when they hear the wacky and over the top, "Henry Whitter's Fox Chase."

"Old Time Corn Shuckin'" by the Blue Ridge Corn Shuckers is a funny moonshine exploitation number featuring several players soloing on their stringed instruments whilst verbally claiming to be tipping the 'ol jug. The two LP set is brought to a dramatic and foot stomping end by real-life preacher Alfred G. Karnes bellowing "I Am Bound For the Promised Land" while slapping the holy dog shit out of the loosely strung strings on his rare Gibson harp/guitar.

The Original CARTER FAMILY "Legendary Performances" RCA. LP.

On one hand, I'm humbled trying to think of something original I can say about the original Carter family that hasn't been said a jillion times before. On the other hand I realize how ignorant American humanoids in our day and age are when it comes to knowing about the roots of popular music. It can't be repeated too many times that the Carters and Jimmie Rodgers (and a few others you could count on one hand) were as significant to the kick starting of the country music industry as Henry Ford was to the automobile and Ray Kroc was to the great American tradition of stuffing your face with fast food.

This album includes a dozen of the very best of a massive catalog of material recorded over the years by Sara, A.P. and Maybelle Carter. "Wildwood Flower" "Keep on the Sunny Side" "Jimmie Brown the Newsboy" and my favorite: "Single Girl Married Girl." Today's casual fans may know Mother Maybelle best as June's ma. Her legacy as a finger pickin' guitar stylist imitated by literally hundreds of later artists far outstrips that role.

A.P. Carter was a humble hillbilly with a musical knack who'd tramp all over the hills for days and even weeks in search of songs for the trio to record. Sara's strong yet unpretentious voice was perfect for the kind of melancholy, wistful or even tragic songs that suited folks during the great depression. Whereas Jimmie the Kid was received by the early country music recording audience as a ladies man who was equally at home in the city or country, the Carters were mountain folk plain and simple. There were no songs in their portfolio about shagging girls. Whereas Rodgers recorded only one religious song in his life (a duet with Sara!) the Carters were church-going family folk who sang songs they grew up hearing on their home turf Clinch Mountain.

As much as I'm in favor of spreading the word about these pioneers I can't help but cock my left eyebrow in suspicion when I hear about some of the wealthy citified folksters who've cashed in on classic Carter's songs over the years. It meant a lot to the family in their old age to see younger generations expressing interest in their music though, so I'll not go there.

ELTON BRITT "Best of Volume II" (1973) RCA. LP

Britt deserves a place in this book if for no other reason than the fact that he's recorded the finest loving tribute song to a deceased country legend I've ever heard "The Jimmie Rodgers Blues." He lets Jimmie's song titles tell most of the story accompanied by some over the top mournful yodeling. He sure as hell wasn't a one hit wonder though, he had a career that lasted a few decades.

On the lead off track "Chime Bells" Britt belts out an impressive sonic orgy of happy yodeling that finishes neck in neck with even ol' Slim Whitman's best. The 1950's was perhaps the best time period of the 20th century for melancholy music. Britt proudly hangs in there with even the biggest names in the music biz with his country flavored pop renditions of standards "Mockingbird Hill" and "Detour." Considering his huge talents Is it just my imagination or is the memory of Elton Britt fading way the hell too quickly?

Perhaps he was an outsider who ran afoul of the Acuff-Opry management clique. I'm not an investigative reporter, just an opinionated jackass with an inquiring mind. I smell a rat. Perhaps Britt was swept under the same rug they've tried to bury Webb Pierce under. Either way he was loaded with talent and deserves a spot on the record rack of any true country music fan.

GRANDPA JONES "28 Greatest Hits" King CD

At the risk of sounding like one of those old TV ads, do you know how much dough you'd have to shell out to find these songs on vinyl? Worse yet it would take you an incredible amount of time to round up even half of them. Grandpa was a mighty man when it came to pickin' and singin' and telling lovable corny jokes, but not very many of his records sold all that many copies. Which makes it even harder to try to find his stuff in that format.

There's no need to of course unless you're one of the handful of CD haters left out there. This is an example of the advent of the compact disc being a tremendous service to humanity. Of all the artists covered in this book I'd have to rank ol' Grandpa as the king of making happy sounding music. Most of his best songs are pure hillbilly humor delivered without apology.

The music is mostly up tempo bluegrass that give the songs a refreshing, and honest edge. How can anybody but a sourpuss carpetbagger not get a laugh at "How Many Biscuits Can You Eat?" My favorite personally is the immortal "Old Rattler" which isn't about a damned snake, he's a coon dog. Rattler appears in a follow up tune too: "Old Rattler's Tree'd Again". "Are You From Dixie" is perhaps the jolliest, button bustin' salute to the great south ever recorded. "I'm My Own Grandpa" is a complex song to follow if you're tipping a jug whilst listening. It proves how influential Grandpa was to later novelty song specialists. "15 cents Is All I Got" is a complete hick comedy routine about the wonders of an indoor toilet within the framework of a song.

Grandpa had a serious side too. He sang in gospel quartets including one on Hee Haw that sold tons of records. He also performed plenty of bluegrass standards as part of his live shows. The versions of "Mountain Dew" and "Our Fathers Had Religion" included on this disc aren't as likely to make you slap your thigh as "Bald Headed End of the Broom," but they have their place.

The HOOSIER HOT SHOTS "Sing Hound Dog" Viking Records. LP .

This act dates back to the 1930's, but this album (which appears to have been pressed in the early 1960's) is the only recording I have by them. That's my failure. I wish I had their complete works. This is definitely one of the most unique acts of all time. At times their musical sound is hillbilly oriented with a fiddle leading the way. At other times a clarinet (!?) takes over.

Sometimes corny humor ala Spike Jones is at the forefront of their sound and at other times I think this must be a white-hick version of R&B's Treniers. The title track "Hound Dog" is worth the price of admission alone, but so is their version of Western classic, "Rye Whiskey" "Them Hillbillies is Mountain Willies Now" is another memorable track. Side two ends up with versions of traditional numbers "Home on the Range" "On Top of Old Smokey" and "Red River Valley". I kept expecting them to cut up on these numbers, but they're sung straight in a folky manner. There's little I like more than a musical aggregation that keeps me on my toes like the Hoosier Hot Shots do with this album.

JIMMIE RODGERS "Country Music Hall of Fame" (1962) RCA. LP.

Rodgers of course is credited with being the first grand poobah of the sales charts from the ranks of what we now call "country" music singers. There were plenty of acts around at the same time singing similar songs. What made Jimmie Rodgers stand out? To me a lot of the hillbilly singers of Jimmie's era sound a bit churchy and stiff; others sound like plain old average pig farmers. Jimmie's voice is neither too starched or too mush mouthed. His image was that of a well-mannered tomcat; a womanizer, but a gentleman just the same. He may have been a playboy, but he sang a lot of songs about loving Mother and missing the family hearth, which seems to have evened things out. He sang about the joys of traveling free all over the country at a time in which many family's had kinfolk wandering around. That made Jimmie Rodgers a sort of surrogate cousin to a lot of folks.

Babe Ruth was enjoying his greatest years during the years of Jimmie's success 1927-1933. I can easily picture in my mind the two of them quaffing back bootleg liquor swapping dirty stories in some fancy deluxe whorehouse. Americans obviously didn't mind their hero's being regular guys back then. After Jimmie passed away there was no one to fill his shoes for many years. Even though eventual behind the scenes power monger Roy Acuff did all he could to re-write history and anoint himself as "King" of country it's obvious that in spite of his talents he simply didn't have the same magic or broad appeal as Rodgers.

This particular collection is blessed with a string of fine cowboy songs that are fairly hard to find in any format: "When the Cactus is In Bloom" "Cowhand's Last Ride" and "Yodeling Cowboy." "Sweet Mama Hurry Home or I'll Be Gone" is one of his absolute best numbers. It's a great example of the fact that in spite of Jimmie's cornball hat and bow tie, a lot of his songs are just loaded with attitude. "I'm Free From the Chain Gang Now" is a moving song in the same spirit of those sung by Rodger's fans Haggard and Cash in later years.

The stunning "T.B. Blues" is appropriately the final track. One of the most incredible songs of the 20th century, Jimmie sings about his rapidly approaching death. I've heard it a hundred times... and I still say "HOLY SHIT!" out loud when he gets to the part about the graveyard being a lonesome place. Anybody who thinks '60's rock lyricists broke new ground with their uninhibited lyrics should take a listen to it.

JIMMIE RODGERS "Jimmie the Kid" (1961) RCA. LP.

This album fits well with the others I've singled out for this book. Plenty of Tom cattin' numbers can be found here such as the title track "Jimmie the Kid" which is in the same spirit as "Man of the Road" by present day great Wayne Hancock.

"Blue Yodel #12 (Barefoot Blues)" and "Blue Yodel #2 (My Lovin' Gal Lucille)" and "Memphis Yodel" all send me to tipping my flask every time too. The Rodger's standard that inspired an Elvis Presley movie "Frankie and Johnnie" is included. A jillion other singers have covered it too.

We're treated with Mrs. Rodger's alleged favorite recording by her hubby "Home Call" which is a happy tune about Jimmie at home with his wife and daughter on any given evening at his Texas home the "Blue Yodeler's Paradise".

"Mother Queen of My Heart" concerns (according to the liner notes) "The Gambling Phase of Man's Weakness." From the perspective of us fans here in the next century it also seems to be a milestone you can trace a lot of morality songs by guys like Hank Sr. and Porter Wagoner and Red Sovine (to name but a few) back to.

JIMMIE RODGERS "My Rough and Rowdy Ways" RCA. LP.

Music families like the Carter's often sang songs that referred to "lost" kinfolk who had wandered off away from home. Jimmie Rodgers songs were more often than not from the perspective of the wanderer; the hobo riding the rails or an inter-state playboy keeping one eye on the local yocal cuties and one eye open for the law. Songs about far off places and the gals left behind there. The 20th century American concept of hop in the car and GO MAN GO can be traced back all the way to the singing brakeman and train songs.

One LP can't possibly cover all the necessary Rodgers tracks that you need, much less cover what you'd like to have. This one is loaded though. No less than three of his "Blue Yodels" are here including "#1," "T for Texas" "#9" "Standin' on the Corner" and his final Blue Yodel: "The Women Make a Fool Out Of Me." "Mule Skinner Blues" (alright… technically Blue Yodel #8) and the hep jazz number "Blue Eyed Jane" are here too. "In the Jailhouse Now #2," "Peach Picking Time in Georgia" hell, you get the idea. RCA pulled out all the stops on this album. Like I say though, once you catch on to Jimmie and begin to understand him like he's a long lost relative speaking to you through your very soul, you'll run out like I did and buy anything with his name on it

.

JIMMIE RODGERS "The Essential" (1997) RCA. CD.

For years and years I struggled with frustrating Rodger's vinyl LP's with repetitive tracks, alternate song titles and secondary sound quality. This problem was solved appropriately the day of my first pilgrimage to Jimmie's official museum in his hometown of Meridian, Mississippi. The answer to my prayers was in the gift area: 20 tracks, Jack… digitally re-mastered and lovingly selected.

I've got scores of record albums and CDs of singer's so-called "essential" hits; this time RCA actually pulled it off. "T for Texas" "In the Jailhouse Now" "California Blues" "Pistol Packin' Mama" "Muleskinner Blues" "T.B. Blues "etc, etc. It's LOADED. The sound quality is good enough that it seems easier for friends of mine who are addicted to modern new-fangled production standards to get into Jimmie.

I don't need a crowd of yahoo's around hand clappin' and jaw jackin' when it's time to hang out with Jimmie for a few hours. All you need is yourself, a boom box and a roaring campfire in a remote spot at night with the stars shining; oh… and of course a half gallon of Jim Beam. Crank this baby up and stare into the fire. Take a few hits off of your jug… imagine that Jimmie is seated next to you on a log singing for the two of you. If you're LUCKY you'll find yourself connecting with the Grandpappy of country music in a personal way. If you open up he'll become as real to you as a relative who died before you had a chance to meet 'em. Try it...I did.

SPADE COOLEY "Mr. Music Himself : Volume 3" LP.

You don't hear too many folks even in knowledgeable circles of country music fans talking about Spade Cooley. It's easy to figure… after all, he murdered his wife and spent the rest of his life in prison. The man committed a crime and paid his debt to society.

Since he passed away long ago I don't see any reason why we shouldn't all just remember him for his great music, at least what we can find, that is. It's a textbook fact that Spade invented the term Western Swing and presided as it's first self-appointed monarch thereof.

This album has what sounds like two mostly complete radio shows. There's an incredible stew of sounds to be heard here. Cooley was able to blend a country fiddle band sound with the pep of a big band, the frisky, happy rhythms of polka and a smattering of early rock and roll.

"Rye Straw" is a great fiddle tune that shows off Spade's personal instrumental talents. "Little Brown Jug," and "Rock Around the Clock" make good use of a horn section. "Breaking Up Party" and "Butterfingers" employs a female singer with a friendly, sexy voice. "Clarinet Polka" finds me dancing around the room in my underwear with a string of Polish sausage's for a crown.

This album is only the tip of the iceberg. Spade was talented as hell. It's time for his recordings to be as available as the tired contemporary crap on the shelves at Wal-Mart.

SPADE COOLEY "Spadella" (1994) Columbia Records. CD.

A happy update on the Spade Cooley front: just before my last edit of this final edition of this book, I found this great collection of twenty studio tracks by Spade and his orchestra. These numbers were recorded between 1944 and 1946. Highlights include snappy dance instrumentals such as "Oklahoma Stomp" "Swingin' the Devils Dream" "Cow Bell Polka" and a 1946 entrant to the first R&R song sweepstakes: "Three Way Boogie" with accordions rocking it up as opposed to saxes or guitars.

The primo vocal cuts (featuring veteran Tex Williams) are "I've Taken All I'm Gonna Take From You" "Detour" and a track just used for a 2010 film of a Jim Thompson book ("The Killer Inside Me") "Shame on You." The song is featured prominently serving as a means of scolding a psychopath Deputy who kills a few gals out in West Texas. Spade is really back with a bang.

12. ROCKABILLIES AND HEP CATS

BILL HALEY "From Western Swing to Rock" Proper Records. 4 CDs.

It is clear that Bill Haley was a huge fan of Hank Sr. like so many other musicians of his generation. The first song on the first disc of this set is a cover of "Too Many Parties Too Many Pals." As an up and coming player in ham and egg country bands he could yodel like nobody's business as heard here in "Cotton Haired Gal," and in the over the top, "A Yodelers Lullaby." I bet Hank himself would've been impressed; perhaps he heard Haley's Four Aces of Western Swing band and dug it.

Hank left the planet just before Haley found just the right hot players for his ongoing Saddlemen band and had a huge hit with "Crazy Man Crazy" spanning lines between genres. Would Hank have smacked his fist on the bar and grinned if he had somehow survived to hear "Rock Around the clock"?

I think Haley and Hank were heading in the same direction. Mr. Williams would probably have rocked up some of his music if he had gone on to have a lengthy career. Put that in your pipe and smoke it, food for thought.

Getting back to the recordings compiled for this must have collection, let's focus on disc one well before he amalgamated rock. Haley wins me over with his ranch-style crooning compared to some of the lame, popular movie stars. Autry and Roy R. have always left me a bit cold. They seem to be singing to children. A lot of it seems squeaky clean and pussy like in a similar way to the non-threatening rap, cowpoke, dude-ranch duds of today.

Haley purrs like he's gonna nail "My Sweet Little Gal From Nevada." He had heard blues singers on the road for years and played beer halls in his stomping grounds of Chester, PA. that were crammed to the gills with Philly shipyard sailors who were horny as they were loud and drunk.

This four CD set is a fascinating look at the progression of Haley's various musical aggregations over the years. The band that became so famous for "inventing" rock and roll (that topic is discussed elsewhere) is a tight, talented unit with skills that crossed genres just like Bob Wills bands. He learned the ropes playing country music and deserves a spot in this book.

BOOGIE WOOGIE FEVER" Compilation Charly Records. LP.

This album is well stocked with great hard to find songs pristinely mastered for your fanny swinging or rug cuttin' pleasure. Boogie-woogie is Rockabilly's slightly older but lesser known cousin. It's country music with a pumping beat, without the hiccupy vocals or dominant frantic guitars that came along later. Still, I'm hard pressed to do much less than spit beer in your face if you're a rockabilly fan and you claim these songs don't pull your chain.

This is a perfectly compiled sixteen-song treasure trove. "Barracuda" by Cliffie Stone gets things started in an up tempo and irresistible way. You just can't go wrong with a catchy fish song. Up next is Tennessee Ernie Ford who seconds the motion with "Catfish Boogie." This one and his other two tunes included here "Blackberry Boogie," and "Shotgun Boogie" are wild and raucous. They are about as far removed as it gets from his later "Pea Pickin' material which of course is as impossible to dance to as a William Shatner narration.

Gene O'Quin ("Texas Boogie" and "Boogie Woogie Fever") sounds amazingly like current boogie-woogie master Wayne Hancock. He too is a native of Dallas, Texas. Ramblin' Jimmie Dolan's manic "Hot Rod Race" is of course a keeper. Merle Travis and even the Louvin Brothers are to be found on this LP as well.

Yeah, yeah, it'd be great to have pristine 78s or 45s of these songs but fat chance of that happening. You're better off seeking this compilation out and saving your money for beer.

CARL MANN "In Rockabilly Country" Charlie Records U.K. LP.

I bought this record as a Rockabilly fanatic over 20 years ago, before I had developed a proper appreciation for country music. I was a bit disappointed back then that Carl was merely singing country music in a Jerry Lee Lewis 70's style as opposed to rocking up Nat King Cole songs like he did in his earlier days. So, this record received one sad playing or so per year until I eventually I came to one of the great realizations of my life while walking out of a Jerry Lee concert later in the 80's. I had gone to see the killer sing "Whole Lotta Shakin'" and "Breathless" and "Great Balls of Fire". He sang those songs just fine, but the numbers he had really poured his talents into that had likewise moved me, were slower country numbers like "What Made Milwaukee Famous" and "Middle-aged Crazy". HHmmm.

Not long after my friend Mike McNally (who had exposed me to rockabilly as a tender teenager) and I had a drunken experience in which we spun "Lonely Blue Boy" by Conway Twitty over and over and over instead of the usual up tempo rockers we usually played. I began to realize and accept the fact I was looking at "slow" country music differently.

One night, after drinking a few tumblers of Jim Beam I worked up the courage to admit to myself that George Jones best song was not "White Lightnin," after all. Soon after I figured out that "Teenage Boogie," is sure as hell not Webb Pierce's best.

Over the years I began to properly appreciate this album, which is loaded with fine songs utilizing Carl's voice which is similar in ways to that of my fellow Texan Dale Watson. "Bull of the Woods" and "Gonna Drink a Little Beer" are the honky tonkers included and they are really great. "Blue Eyes

Cryin' in the Rain" has been covered by a jillion singers, but Carl's is one of the best. "Nobody Knows How the Singer Feels" and "When the Leaves Have Turned All Brown" are delivered with such professionalism you've gotta figure ol' Carl spent his post Sun Records years playing taverns and juke joints in the south. He aged like fine wine. I wish he had taken as visible a place as his old Phillips International label cohort Charlie Rich.

COLLINS KIDS "The Rockin Rollin' Collins Kids" (1981) Bear Family. LP.

Couch potatoes may remember sister Lorrie Collins from a few ancient 1950's "adventures of Ozzie and Harriet" TV shows. She played a love interest for teen heart throb Rickie Nelson and even dueted with him in the end of show musical segments. Even though Rickie's career was going great guns at the time and he was obviously the much bigger star at the time in retrospect Lorrie and her child prodigy guitar slinger little brother Larry, left behind a pile of red hot rockabilly recordings that makes even Nelson's best sound pitiful by comparison.

Don't fault Ricky. Damn few of the studs of the Sun label stable left behind anywhere near a batch of superior sides like the Collins Kids did. The gimmick was this: Larry was still a child but able (thanks to the tutelage of one of the worlds best players Joe Maphis) to play burning guitar leads on a double neck that paced tunes Lorrie would sing lead on. Both siblings joined together on the choruses creating some stunning harmonies hick accents and all.

The Collins Kids were part of the same west coast country music scene that included the Maddox Family who were also playing balls out rockabilly before the genre was supposedly born in the south and east. Some of the earlier tunes on this album: “The Cuckoo Rock” the “Beetle Bug Bop” and the “Rockaway Rock” are certainly amongst the first wave of American rock and roll songs. The Kids definitely had one foot firmly rooted in country though. There are plenty of old TV footage clips of the Kids on stage in California with Merle Travis, Tex Ritter, Johnny Bond and others. As the 1950’s rolled along and the kids got older their music only got better spear headed by Larry’s progress as a guitarist. “Hoy Hoy” and “Just Because” are amazing up tempo show stoppers that had to have impressed even Nelson’s hired gun picker, James Burton.

Any collection of Collins Kids songs is bound to be good, but the German Bear Family label as usual has dug a little deeper than the competition and presented a whopping sixteen essential tracks on pristine Euro-vinyl.

ELVIS PRESLEY “The Sun Sessions” RCA. LP.

Even though he’s always thought of in terms of being the “King” of rock and roll for a good while at the beginning of his career he was considered a country chart artist. When Elvis, Scotty and Bill first gigged around the southern states there wasn’t a “rock and roll” club circuit to play to promote their releases for Sam Phillips mighty Sun Records.

Playing black R&B clubs was out of the question and frankly the boys were probably too hick for most northern pop audiences. They just naturally were booked to play country music oriented events often touring as part of a package show including acts ranging from the Carters to Webb Pierce. From the start the jumped-up arrangements of the material and Elvis stage moves of course set them apart from the other acts they played with.

Initially the boys played early on the bill in package shows, but it wasn't long before it became impossible for even the most popular country veterans to follow Elvis on stage. This really hacked some of them off evidently; imagine how humiliating it felt for men like Webb to be eventually driven to actually record a song like "Teenage Boogie" to try to keep hold of the huge portion of the country audience that was jumping on to the rock and roll band wagon. The eventual mass popularity of Elvis and rock and roll eventually almost killed off country music. Sales figures plummeted. We shouldn't blame poor Elvis for that though. The world was changing and just like country music had slowly been modifying from the days of Jimmie Rodgers it was time for it to change some more.

Elvis grew up a simple country boy and even though his musical tastes included a wide variety of singers ranging from Dean Martin and Wynonie Harris, he never turned heel on country music, he just goosed it in the ass.

The songs on this constantly in print album such as "Blue Moon of Kentucky" "Milkcow Blues Boogie" "That's All Right Mama" and "Mystery Train" have been described by many egghead music writers as rock and roll's definitive recordings.

A listen to the songs confirms what a mighty influence the country greats Elvis and the boys grew up listening to on the radio had on what they created. They quit playing country music extravaganzas soon after Elvis was signed to RCA. But Elvis never forsook his country roots to his dying day. Years later in a different phase of his career Presley songs like "In the Ghetto" and "Kentucky Rain" inspired a whole new generation of country singers.

Old timers who used to think Elvis was squirrely and no good back in the 50's probably feel differently today; they probably consider these songs a treat to listen to considering all the hogdip that's been trowled out over the years.

GEORGE JONES "Rockin' the Country" (1985) Mercury. LP.

A re-issue album entirely devoted to George's 1958-1961 rockabilly recordings. Of course the humongous crossover pop/country hit "White Lightnin'" is here along with a lesser known song intended to capitalize off of its success "Revenuer Man." "Slave Lover" is a funny novelty number George himself wrote about being pussy whipped into submission. "Who Shot Sam" is even more moonshine fueled decadence you can't help but enjoy. There aren't any ballads here, just hick humor songs with cracking guitar leads and George Jones amiable vocals.

Incidentally I know from observing my misguided non-country music loving friends over the years that these songs really do appeal to a lot of rock and roll fans. Quite possibly George could have made more money in the 1960's if he had stuck to recording pop music. I'm glad he didn't though. Just think of all the classic country songs he wouldn't have sung? You can bet the suits would've eventually had him covering pop "treasures" of the day like the latest Chad and Jeremy or Herman's Hermits number...YUCK!

HARDROCK GUNTER "Gonna Rock 'n Roll Gonna Dance All Night" Roller Coaster Records U.K. CD.

This man has a mighty though unfortunately largely unnoticed claim to fame. At a point in time in which Hank Williams Sr. was very much alive and all over the charts he beat Ike Turner (with Jackie Brenston), Bill Haley, Elvis Presley and everybody else to the punch with arguably the first really popular song that both used the phrase: "rock and roll" and sounded like full blown rompin' stompin' rock and roll.

The song was titled "Gonna Dance All Night" and as if that isn't impressive enough it should be pointed out that it wasn't Hardrock's first single. That was an equally wild and wooly boogie woogie number known as the "Birmingham Bounce." It became a huge hit especially in the south. This information is important to we country music fans for a couple reasons at least. First off, Mr. Gunter (who still performs as of this writing at the age of 78) can claim a big share of the glory of kick starting rock and roll in the name of country music.

Some well meaning folks argue that all the credit should go to R&B performers of the era, but that's too simplistic an explanation. It's not the purpose of this book to rehash the question of the true roots of rock and roll. Entire books have been written on that subject already. I'm saying listen to the earliest songs on this CD; look at the dates they were released. Holy Shit! Hardrock Gunter deserves a helluva lot of credit he's never received.

That's only the beginning of the story of the songs on this loaded 31 song CD issued in the UK. The flip side of "Birmingham Bounce" was a solid Ernest Tubb style ballad "How Can I Believe You Love Me" which is followed on the

CD by a post-war military humor number “Rifle Belt & Bayonet.

Next Hardrock provides an answer (complete with appropriate steel guitar licks) for Hank’s “My Buckets Got a Hole in it” with the great “My Buckets Been Fixed”. As the ‘50’s rocked along and some country artists faded out of the picture, Gunter recorded a slew of sometimes spooky, echo drenched rockabilly numbers such as: “Jukebox Help Me Find My Baby” and “Whoo I Mean Whee” that have obviously influenced modern day musicians (the Cramps come to mind--they had to be big fans of Hardrock Gunter).

Gunter tried his hand at several more very different styles over the years. “I'll Go Chasin’ Women” and “Mountain Dew” are just two from a 1958 album’s worth of salty hillbilly humor songs where the main emphasis is on his funny hick vocalizin’. Instrumentals “Hardrock Rocks the Moon” and “Tico Tico” should appeal to fans of Merle Travis and the dozens of country guitar pickers in his wake.

There’s never a dull moment on this CD. Like I've said elsewhere in this book, if you had to go out and find all these songs on vinyl it’d cost you a fortune since many of them are extremely obscure… which is a damn shame in itself.

It’s about damned time Hardrock Gunter was recognized by the mainstream music press in this country for his contributions. This is another shameful instance in which folks in Europe and around the world appreciate one of our native talents better than most Americans do.

HASIL ADKINS “What the Hell was I Thinking” Fat Possum . CD.

In spite of the fact that this was released on a blues label and aside from the fact that Hasil was one of rock and roll's most notorious wild men, this is indeed a country album.

West Virginia's favorite son starts off the album with "Your Memories" slowly strumming his guitar and singing in the most wistful voice I've ever heard him croon in. By track two he's left the introspective mood behind. The song is an Adkins favorite "Ugly Woman" in which he bemoans in a tongue in cheek manor the miseries of having the most beauty challenged shall we say gal in town.

He strums along on his acoustic adding occasional one-man-band percussive sounds. "Beautiful Hills" finds Hasil singing and strumming sounding a lot like the folks from the hills a couple hundred miles south around Bristol, Virginia back in the 1920's (see the "Bristol Sessions" album review). This is a bit out of character for a man who was known for singing about nailin' gal's heads to the wall of his cabin.

"Somehow You'll Find Your Way" is a nice peaceful number that's pure authentic country like the Carters used to sing. It's sure as hell more country in the traditional sense than 98% of what was played on your commercial psuedo-country radio station this week. Hell, make that 100%.

Adkins gets real, real gone a couple times or so on this CD too. "Up On Mars" and "Gone Gone Gone" would likely send a purist sourpuss like Roy Acuff clamoring for his Rolaids and Preparation H. Fact is though Hasil was a man who lived in the mountains all his life. He's as much a bona fide product of his American rural roots as any other musician. Ask his legions of fans in places like Sweden; to them he is the prototypical U.S. citizen.

JERRY LEE LEWIS "Boogie Woogie Country Man" (1975) Mercury Records. LP.

This LP displays the Killer's versatility damn well. The songs range from a revival meeting stomp; "Jesus Is on the Main Line" and the dignified Stuart Hamblen classic "(Remember Me) I'm the One Who Loves You" to a sleazy pair of honky tonk numbers penned by Tom T. Hall "Red Hot Memories (Ice Cold Beer)" and "I Can Still Hear the Music in the Rest Room." All throughout of course Jerry Lee shows a lot of personality such as his snide remarks that compliment songs "Thanks For Nothing" and the title track "Boogie Woogie Country Man" wherein he romps and stomps across the keys in showoff mode whilst declaring himself the cock of the damned walk musically speaking.

JERRY LEE LEWIS "Complete Palomino Cub Recordings" 2 CDs.

As great as Jerry Lee's studio work has been throughout his career if you want the real Killer and no filler, you've got the choice between this two CD set, or you're gonna have to find him out on the road some night at a smoke filled honky tonk.

I've seen him play live at huge civic centers and theaters in front of thousands of people who were primarily there to see him sing his '50's rock and roll hits. I had a good enough time at those shows I suppose, but I never really saw what he can do until I lucked out and saw him at the very club the songs on this collection were recorded at in North Hollywood.

Jerry Lee is plainly inhibited by all the rules and bullshit that go along with state fair and concert hall gigs. Hell, people even bring their kids out to shows like that. He's much more at home in front of a few hundred drunks guzzling outta longnecks. To hell with "rules; to hell with set lists. To hell with going over all the old hits for the zillionth time. I want to see Jerry Lee sing whatever the hell he feels like singing at the moment and luckily on his best nights that's what he wants to do. Only when he's totally uninhibited and comfortable as during the shows this material was recorded at do you hear the man at his best.

This is the same man who recorded what a lot of folks besides your humble author feel is the best live rock and roll album of all time (the "Live in Hamburg" LP). It shouldn't come as a big surprise that he's the head honcho of live country music too.

Disc one starts off with a playful version of Hank's "You Win Again". Jerry Lee is in good humor. He's changing every other word around making it more adult and steamy than Hank ever sang it. He sets up "What Made Milwaukee Famous" with one of his most memorable quotations ever concerning booze: "if the lord made anything better he kept it for himself."

He adds that Jimmy Lee Swaggert, his TV evangelist cousin probably knows that's the truth. Jerry Lee is going to hell along with the beer drunk, chain-smoking, lustful crowd that cheered him on at the wicked Palomino Club. We probably are too, for listening to this and enjoying it so much.

A couple songs later Lewis brays out the smutty "Meat Man" and I reflect how fellow pianist Anton Lavey himself might have approved. "Big Legged Woman" keeps the crowd roaring and then things slow down while Jerry Lee cranks a couple mandatory '50's rock hits on his own terms. Next, time for a couple melancholy numbers "Bottles and Barstools" and the moving "Who's Gonna Play This Old Piano."

The 42 songs on the two discs show an incredible versatility on Jerry Lee's part and he's aided and abetted by some great musicians including the legendary James Burton and Kenny Lovelace. You can only get into the flow of these songs when you come around to realizing it's best to not expect note for note arrangements you are familiar with. Lewis decides on the spot how faithful he wants to stay to the songs.

He leers like a horny lecher on "Chantilly Lace" yet sounds almost overwhelmed emotionally singing the simple words to "You Are My Sunshine." To close out disc two, the Killer gazes at Hank Williams Sr.'s vision of hell: "Picture From Life's Other Side" before closing with a wistful version of "Over the Rainbow" that's enough (when accompanied by a sufficient number of Jim Beam shots) to send hot tears running down even my jaded cheeks.

KINGS OF ROCKABILLY Vol. I Ace Records U.K. 10" vinyl.

There's rockabilly records with a lot of "billy" right up front and then there's citified rockabilly with more beat and guitar pyrotechnics. This collection issued around 1980 or so has some of my favorite rockabilly songs sung by obvious hicks.

"Shadow My Baby" by Glenn Barber is a rustic tale of a two-timin' trollop. "I'm Gonna Tell" by Cousin Louie is as country as Goober Pyle's bumpkin cat clothes. The immortal "Wine-o-Boogie" by Bill Nettles (occasionally sung by Wayne Hancock live) isn't a rockabilly song at all really. File it under hillbilly boogie alongside Tennessee Ernie Ford's great boogie-woogie songs.

The lyrics to Eddie Burke's "Rock Mop" are unabashedly hayseed. Rather than bragging about being a cool cat like city-billy singers he sings about his gal walloping him over the head with a mop, which leads to him dancing with the stinkin' thing for kicks. "Spin the Bottle" by the mighty Benny Joy isn't an urban hipster tune about scoring or getting loaded, it's about a teen clodhopper party where if you're lucky you might get kissed by a purty gal.

Personally, I love a lot of billy in my rockabilly just like I prefer sweet tea. As you might expect, I've practically worn out my copy of this album over the last 30 years.

LEON RUSSELL "Hank Wilson's Back. Volume I" Shelter Records. LP.

Just as the Eagles were picking up stream with their hippie oriented sound (which makes me wretch) Leon Russell was issuing this fine, fine traditional album that proved that the entire generation hadn't lost it's senses. This is probably the best country album issued by a performer associated with longhair rock and roll during the period of hippie record chart dominance that extended from the late '60's through the late 1970's.

Leon croons on this LP versions of both Hank Sr. and George Jones songs close to as well as just about anybody else ever has. Hot dog! "She Thinks I Still Care" "The

Window Up Above" "I'm So Lonesome I Could Cry" are all so simply beautiful it's no wonder everybody from Billy Byrd to Melba Montgomery to Pete Wade and Johnny Gimble are heard throughout this album.

All the hippie rockers who thought they were "improving" country music by cranking out retarded nasal tripe like the aforementioned Eagles were fooling themselves. They strayed too far from what country music is all about. Don't talk to me in negative terms about the commercial excesses of country these days and then crow about how great hogwash like "New Kid in Town" or "Let Your Love Flow" by the mellow-hippie Bellamy Brothers was back in the day. When hippies and suburban airhead models and jocks sing country It sucks--yesterday, today and tomorrow. Most importantly, it's not country music. Go file it with all the other nauseating soft rock records of the '70's.

13. TRUCKERS

COMMANDER CODY & His Lost Planet Airmen "Hot Licks, Cold Steel" (1972) LP.

Appearances can be deceiving. Even though the year this was recorded was 1972 and even though judging by the back album cover photo it's obvious some of these boys had long-ass hair, this isn't just another rock band pretending to play country music. Take a closer look at that band photo. Commander Cody's filled his stage with a full band including a permanent pedal steel player, piano and part time fiddler. Add to that Bill Kirchen who is a bona fide A#1 guitar genius leading the guitar section and you've got a helluva band.

This album is chock full of great truck driving songs like "Truckstop Rock" "Looking At the World Through a

Windshield" and an all time favorite of every knight of the road I know "Truck Drivin' Man." "Mama Hated Diesels" is a slow story song done to perfection. "Kentucky Hills of Tennessee" may be goofy enough to give you the idea these boys had a collective weird sense of humor, but they never sing like they're looking down on the men behind the wheel or rural folk in general. They're having fun obviously. I bet when these guys showed up at certain country venues they caught a lot of heat from Joe six-pack types for looking like hippies, but once they started playing, I'm sure even those good 'ol boys eventually turned to waving beer cans in the air instead of fists.

DAVE DUDLEY "Listen Betty I'm Singing Your Song" (1970) Mercury Records. LP.

Subject wise a sad, sort of broken down Dudley album. The songs seem to be from the viewpoint of a trucker whose had enough and is throwing in the damned towel. "Farewell to the Road" and "The Rollin's All Gone Out of This Rollin' Stone" both make this point clear.

It seems like the first song on side one "Listen Betty (I'm Singing Your Song)" is a pay back of an old promise at the end of a long career. "I Feel a Cry Coming On" and "Down on Whiskey Row" have me even worrying a bit about Dave until I realize he's a singer and not a trucker in the first damn place. I'm glad he included the happy tribute to a local drinking joint "Six-o-One" on the album to brighten things up a bit even so.

There's no doubt this is Dudley in a subdued mode compared to his cock-of-the-walk trucker persona albums. He does a helluva job with songs penned by some real heavyweights including two by Tom T. Hall and "For the Good Times" by Kris Kristofferson.

Pete Drake's steel guitar dominates musically on this LP, whereas in the past it was the twangy six-string guitar. That's fine with me; it doesn't suit a great talent like D.D. to limit himself to one style of song.

DAVE DUDLEY "Truck Drivin' Son of a Gun" (1964) Mercury Records. LP

This classic LP is to truck driving song albums what Krispy Kreme's are to all the other doughnuts out there. Dave Dudley is the big stud, the cock of the walk, the bull of the woods and the yard stick by which all other singers of this sub-genre of country music have been judged for many years.

This album wasn't made with music scholars, historians and eggheads in mind. Never the less, if you asked those sort of fella's I bet you they'd agree that songs like "Truck Drivin' Son-of-a-Gun" and "Speed Traps Weigh Stations & Detour Signs" go beyond most songs sung in a saloon to entertain drunks.

They depict the way that working men lived in the middle 20th century in America as well as any book or movie from the period ever did. These are the same sort of manly songs as the tunes Tex Ritter sang about the west. Put this one in a time capsule… OK?

Apart from such lofty cultural significance this album is fun as hell to listen to on a pure entertainment level of course. "I Got Lost" and "Two Six Packs Away" are hilarious classics and "Jackknife" makes me lighten up on the gas peddle whenever I listen to this album when driving. The reverb guitar sound and simple production on this album are so good I once again feel like mailing a box of bricks C.O.D. to all the jerk label dudes in Nashville who've screwed up country music with their over-production. It probably took Mr. Dudley and five or six musicians eight hours to record this masterpiece.

DEL REEVES "Looking at the World Through a Windshield" (1968) UA Records.

When this album was released Dave Dudley and Red Sovine ruled the damn roost as far as truck driving music is concerned. Mr. Reeves covers both of them here repeatedly, yet still manages nicely to carve out his own niche as a topnotch impersonator and song stylist as well.

He recites Sovine's "Giddyup Go" using a Walter Brennan accent. Ok, Fine enough. The closing track is the classic "Phantom 309". Reeves not only uses a stuttering accent for the narration, he pulls out all stops and stutters out the spoken parts by the phantom driver as well as the waiter at the truck stop.

An inside joke? Or a strange sort of overkill? Maybe I need to ask a trucker. Anyway, this album is overloaded with a dozen absolute classic truck driving tunes. Del pulled it off well enough that he's still singing songs like this at Opryland after a lengthy, lucrative career in Las Vegas. Two of my favorites are; "Gear Bustin' Sort Of a Feller" and "You Can't Housebreak a Tomcat." This album raises the eternal question, do I pack a thermos of coffee for this record player run? Or a 12-pack of ice-cold corporate beer... HHmm?

DICK CURLESS "CB Special" (1976) BD Communications. LP.

You'd better grab the mic of your CB and start working it hard as hell if you're gonna find a copy of this one. On this independent label release we are treated to the talents of the greatest bass voice in country music.

Mr. Curless is backed by the perhaps obscure as they are talented Curtis McPeake & the Nashville Pickers. Sounding here at the height of his creative powers, Curless reprises not only his own hit songs such as "Tombstone Every Mile", he also runs through the best known songs of the entire truck driving hymn book from "Six Days on the Road" and "Give Me Forty Acres" to "Convoy" and "Wolf Creek Pass."

I'm mighty partial to his versions here of "Pinball Machine" and "Blazin' Smoke Stack" to name a couple. The entire 20 song album is just about as good as it is hard to find. It's like trying to locate a can of COORS in Maine or Oregon in the mid '70's.

DICK CURLESS "Tombstone Every Mile" (1965) Tower Records. LP.

My nominee's for the biggest, deepest, booming-est, studliest voice in the history of country music: Dick Dudley, Claude Gray, Lee Marvin, Junior Brown, Dick Curless. The envelope please. The winner is, the pride of the friggin' Hainesville woods Dick Curless.

The title song of this album is as hard-boiled as Curless' voice. It's about haulin' "podayda's" along a stretch of road in Maine where the gravestones from vehicle wrecks are like mile markers. Dick's voice is so manly in traditional songs like "Nine Pound Hammer" and "King of the Road" he makes the competition seem sissy like.

In album cover pictures Curless looks big enough to kick sand in Claude Akin's face at the beach, or get away with filling his boots with shaving cream at the truck stop shower room. Even a big guy like Dick has got a sensitive side too that you can hear in softer songs like "Tear Drops in My Heart" and "Heart Talk". Unless Ted Cassidy from "the Adams Family" cut a country LP I don't know about Dick Curless has bragging rights down at his end of the sonic spectrum without a doubt.

JERRY REED "Eastbound and down" (1977) RCA. LP.

Did you like Jerry's role in "Smokey and the bandit?" You'll love this album then. There are three tracks from the film including the title song and the lesser known: "The Bandit" and "The Legend."

I dig the two instrumentals on Side one: "Bake" and "Lightning Rod" which reminds us Jerry is not only a great actor and singer and song writer, what a mighty picker.

Side two begins with the funny "Framed" which carries the road concept along, but for some odd reason Jerry stomps on the brakes and kills the mood with a ballad song sung in an accent free voice "Rainbow Ride." He regains a bit of momentum with a cover of Waylon's "Just To Satisfy You" but oddly ends what began as a blue-collar friendly album you'll want to guzzle Pabst to with a version of a Bob Dylan song "Don't Think Twice It's All Right."

What the hell, an eighty-five percent superb album. Not bad at all.

JIM & JESSE "Diesel on My Tail" (1964) Epic Records. LP.

These aren't the guys you automatically think of when you think of the royal potentates of truck driving music. But what the hell, on this album they tackle a damn infamous collection of road music classics and comport themselves well. Their sound is much more blue-grassy than Dudley or Sovine and the lyrics are delivered straighter than the usually funny Willis Brothers.

This makes for a nice change of pace. The title track "Diesel On My Tail" is an obvious classic. "Lovin' Machine" will have you slappin' your thigh with its double entendre lyrics. "The Ballad of Thunder Road" and "Truck Drivin' Man" and "Girl on the Billboard" are all more than solid cover versions. "Tijuana Taxi" is creatively arranged with a fuzz-tone guitar in the background.

The obvious thing to do with this album is to tape it and store the cassette in your glove compartment or your cluttered dashboard for use as frequent road music.

JIM NESBITT "The Best of" (1971) Chart Records. LP.

Of course not every album in this book is jam packed with 100% equally topnotch songs. If I claimed that I'd be a goddamned liar. This greatest hits package from Chart records humorist (and stable mate of the great Junior

Samples I might add) Jim Nesbitt is essential for the good stuff within.

Nesbitt recorded two superior tracks that are miles beyond the rest of his topical, funny material. "Tiger in My Tank" and "Truck Driving Cat With 9 Lives" are both funny as hell trucker tunes recorded with talented musicians. The rest of Nesbitt's songs seem to pigeonhole him as a small labels answer to Ray Stevens. That's not a bad thing; "Runnin' Bare" is worth a few yucks and seems to pre-date Steven's "The Streak" by a few years.

"When They Sent My Old Lady To the Moon" is a sort of Al Bundy fantasy. "Pollution" is a social conscious tune that devolves in the third verse into an amusing mother-in-law joke. "I'm Yeller" is a rather un-gung-ho Vietnam War song. "Having Fun in '71" is an admission Nesbitt doesn't have the answer to all the hot questions of the day back in the Nixon era.

If I had to guess I'd say he was pushed into writing and recording some "cause oriented" songs by his label. Remember, this was the age of TV's "All in the Family". He's not very profound, but he never claims to be. I wish they had let him sing more truck driver anthems personally. The two on this LP are so good and unique that this album deserves ranking in these pages.

RED SIMPSON "Roll, Truck Roll" (1966) Capitol Records. LP.

Just like there are several different brand trucks on the road there are several styles of truck driving music. Much of it is steeped in blue grass for instance. Red Simpson's truckin' tunes are definitely the cream of the crop of the west coast style sounding songs. Not only has he co-written a lot of songs with the pope of Bakersfield himself Buck Owens, his best albums were released by Capitol Records whose artist roster for years seemed to be a who's who list of west coast country titans such as Wynn Stewart and Merle Haggard.

Red's a different breed of truck driving song singer. When you hear Curless and Dudley you picture big guys with crushing handshakes. I doubt that Simpson ever learned to drink sweet tea or moonshine like the Willis boys or Jim Nesbitt probably did. He seems like a slightly more introspective type of guy… perhaps a Lucky Lager drinker… who wouldn't even need a goofy line of bull to attract the truck stop honeys.

Musically, this album is often just one notch or so slower than rockabilly and the guitar leads rock in an aggressive mid '60's fashion. When he sings "Nitro Express" and "Give Me 40 Acres" and "Six Days on the Road" and other standards he puts his own stamp on the tunes. His voice is a bit raw, but his delivery is relaxed.

Unlike some of his southern brethren, he never oversells the songs in a comic, goofy, cornball manner. "Roll Truck Roll" and "My Baby's Waitin'.." were new anthems heard on this LP first. Side two ends with "Runaway Truck" a Red original with an ironic twist at the end of the tale to nicely close out a dashboard thumpin' album that's as fresh even today as a newly cleaned truck stop deep fryer.

RED SIMPSON "Truck Drivin' Fool" (1968) Capitol Records. LP.

You'd never know there was a war going on or billions of hippies parading the streets of U.S. cities waving signs when this album was recorded. That's fine with me. There were a damned lot of ordinary people back then too busy to protest or attend love-ins or wig out on LSD. A lot of them happened to be truckers. This album would've been perfect for them.

It's hard to worry about what's going on at some university in Ohio or in some jungle 9,000 miles away when you're struggling to simply keep yours eyes open long enough to push your rig home to where your family's waiting. If you're lucky maybe you can spend a day with them before pulling out with another load.

Imagine the comfort Red's voice would be to a poor ol' trucker a couple thousand miles from home on a miserable night with rain pounding on the windshield of his cab. He could laugh along to the ironic humor of "Sleeper 5 X 2" and "Diesel Smoke Dangerous Curves." His thoughts would undoubtedly turn to home during "I'll Be Going Home to Mama" and "Take Me Home." He'd likely be entertained for many miles listening to Red's versions of classics first sung by others such as "A Tombstone Every Mile" and "Jackknife."

There's no hippie flutes or sitars to be heard on this album. There aren't even any "Nashville" style background singers or violins. It's just Red's usually booming voice and a simple combo driven' by a single high-octane guitar picker. This album wouldn't sound nearly as good 35 years later if it had been given a trendy '60's makeover like many an album from this period received. It's timeless, great truck driving music. If you don't like this album you probably don't like country music at all. Put this book down and go find yourself a damned Simon and Garfunkle CD. Good riddance.

RED SOVINE "The Best of" Gusto/Lake Shore Records. 2 LP set.

This is the Sovine collection to have if you can only have one. Fact is, if you do have this and you have the sense God gave a crowder pea, you're gonna want even more. My son and I found a cassette copy of this in a truck stop bargain bin in West Virginia, which also happens to have been Mr. Sovine's home base for many years.

There's twenty tracks on this collection including many standards "Teddy Bear" "Phantom 309" "Little Joe" "Little Rosa" and "Giddy-Up-Go." Expect a few surprises such as Red's take on the blood thirsty Johnny Paycheck tavern fight dittie "Colorado Kool-Aid" and Walter Brennan's syrupy, maudlin hit "Ole Rivers." Red smokes him of course.

All the other songs are good solid ones with one exception; I can do without the Eric Clapton number "Lay Down Sally" which is a bizarre selection. Nineteen songs out of twenty is a pretty damned good positive percentage by my reckoning though.

RED SOVINE "Classic Narration's" (1975) Starday/Gusto. LP.

The world of professional wrestling has nature boy Ric Flair's example to look up to. When it comes to boxing there's Muhammad Ali. If Merle Travis is considered the finest country music guitar picker, than certainly Red Sovine is the king of the "narration" song. Hank Sr. was damn good when it came to spoken word numbers. Porter Wagoner was another obvious master and actor Walter Brennan who couldn't carry a tune in a bucket recorded a jillion of them. But Red "so fine" Sovine is the Sinatra, the Rolex, the Rolls Royce of the recitation, making this a must have album.

Most of these pieces are fairly easy to find, but what makes this album so special of course is having them all together so you can pour a big drink and have a couple hankies handy so you can really submerge yourself into Red's world. Get ready for a steady stream of hard luck stories, crippled children yarns, heart-wrenching tales of dead loved ones and the capper "What Would You Do (If Jesus Came To Your House)."

If Jesus came to my house he'd find this album in the record bin nearest my chair so I could find it easily.

RED SOVINE "Closing Time 'til Dawn" Starday. LP.

Red recorded many concept LP's over the years ranging from truck driving albums to narration collections to gimmick albums in which Red sings accompanied by his cute little Granddaughters. In fact, it's almost a bit of a "novelty" to listen to an album of Red singing straight ahead country songs.

Luckily, he did record a few over the years. This is a durned solid one with about fifty percent blue ribbon winning songs. Side one starts out with the sinful "Whiskey Flavored Kisses" and continues with "Father of Judy Ann" which is a morbid tale in which a father is driven to shoot the feller who impregnated his teenage daughter hence, driving her to suicide. Side two features "Fugitive of Love" and the title track "Closing Time 'til Dawn" which proves Sovine could pull off quite well the sort of lowlife tunes that Johnny Paycheck eventually mastered.

I guess if I had to choose I'd prefer to listen to his truck driving and narration albums, but this record is proof that Red didn't really need to rely on formula's to succeed.

RED SOVINE "Gone But Not Forgotten" Power Pack. CD.

A few years ago I came across an Internet website devoted solely to a fan's memory of hearing the ultimate Red Sovine song on the radio once. The individual responsible for it didn't even own a copy of the song and was damned curious that since it was obviously the quintessential Red Sovine song you'd think it would be on one of his albums. I read the description of the tune and shrugged my shoulders. I hadn't ever heard of a song like that on any of my many Sovine LPs, singles and CDs.

I forgot about that strange website until several months later when the record store I worked at received a handful of Sovine releases we had never carried before.

Lo and behold, just like "Gitty up Go" spotting his old nickname on his long lost dad's license plate, I spotted a song title on the back cover that simply had to be the "lost" song that the website was dedicated to; the ULTIMATE Red Sovine tune.

I bought a copy and rushed home with it after work. The song was every bit as good as the fellow remembered it to be. It was a narrative number about a trucker driving on a lonely highway at night trying to stay awake aided by a jug of coffee and an Elvis tape.

The poor fellow winds up dozing off at the wheel. Suddenly, he finds himself in a brightly lit valley. He climbs out of his truck and see's the King of rock and roll himself in the process of performing a perfect concert using a diamond studded guitar. Angels eventually descend from heaven to place a halo of light on E's head. The driver races to the nearest truck stop to tell someone what he's just seen. Before he has a chance to, he see's from a glance at the headlines of someone's newspaper that King Elvis had passed away the day before.

My description can't possibly do this song justice. Think about it though, then go out and get a copy of this simple eight-song budget CD and listen to "The King's Last Concert." "Does Steppin' Out Mean Daddy Took a Walk" is a nice piece and "Flesh and Blood" is comical due to the overly prudish way it equates a gal being seduced with some sort of twisted crime. But really, "The King's Last Concert" is definitely worth the price of this disc alone.

Whenever I play it I wonder about the poor bastard who wanted a copy of this song so bad he erected a website based on the memory of merely hearing it once. Sadly, just like the brightly lit valley and the angels from heaven above sitting at Elvis's feet listening to him bop away at "Hound Dog" and "Do the Clam" the website has vanished without a trace into cyberspace.

RED SOVINE "Little Rosa" (1960's) Starday. LP.

A damn good assortment of, mid-period Sovine well packaged by Starday. The words "heart rending" are thoughtfully collated over the album title on the front cover. The incredibly sad title track "Little Rosa" features Mr. Sovine chattering away in a daft Italian dialect.

"A Dear John Letter" and "Dream House For Sale" are two more tunes that will leave you in tears unless you're a cold-hearted louse. Red's hit duet with Webb Pierce of "Why Baby Why" is included as well as truck driving staple "Six days on the Road" and the swaggering "King of the Open Road" which is probably the best track on the album.

One of the fun aspects of collecting Red Sovine records is the oddball tunes that turn up occasionally. "Waltzing With Sin" is an incredibly stodgy number that seems to advocate the nut job conservative Christian taboo on dancing. Strangely enough, on the very same album we have: "Sittin' & Thinkin'.." which is a gin fueled tale of debauchery that proves to me Red wasn't really a prig, he was a swinger merely posing as one on the earlier moralistic song. Go figger.

"Old Pipeliner" is both reminiscent of Jimmie Rodgers and a borderline rock and roll song. Damn, another jam packed STARDAY album that is further proof they weren't just a run of the mill tiny little obscure label. They were like a family owned steakhouse that could out serve a chain eatery any day of the week. We need an indie label like that today.

RED SOVINE "Teddy Bear" (1976) Gusto Records. LP.

If albums were ranked on the basis of cover art, this one would be at the tip top. Poor ol' crippled Teddy Bear is seen gazing out the window with his CB mic in hand at a big rig allegedly with Red Sovine himself behind the wheel. I find it helpful when meeting with fellow Red acolytes to judge Mr. Sovine's fantastic catalog of work as we would an on-going pro-wrestling show.

Even though he recorded a lot of two fisted country material his specialty was emotional songs that tug at our heartstrings leaving us misty eyed. On another level just like other masters of melancholy songs (George Jones and Porter Wagoner come to mind) there reaches a point where the story in a narrative tune can become So tragic and saturated with crippled or dead children, pets that sacrifice their lives for their owners and truckers with a heart of gold, you eventually have no choice but to drop your hankie and start slapping your thigh and belly laughing.

Sovine's best albums have songs that are filled with twists and turns that can keep a roomful of people on the edge of their seats. This particular album starts out great with the tragic title track (which has a happy ending) and leads into "Little Rosa" which is a dead child song with no such happy ending in which Red uses that corny Italian accent mentioned in another review.

Unfortunately there follows a few disappointing filler songs that don't induce laughter or weeping no matter how often you play 'em. "Daddy" is a nice remembrance your grandma would love. "Does Steppin' Out Mean Daddy Took a Walk" is a decent broken family song and "18 Wheels Hummin' Home Sweet Home" tips the balance of the album into the "definitely worth getting, but not his best song wise" category.

I've noticed this album cover posted on the walls of record stores all over the country. You better get two copies in case you decide to decorate your den with this legendary drawing of Teddy Bear.

"RIG ROCK DELUXE" (1996) Diesel Only. CD.

I was lucky enough to meet the driving force behind this mighty compilation at a record show in New York City. I immediately realized this collection was so good, I bought multiple copies from him and passed them along to friends.

Anyway, the label honcho was a man named Jeremy Tepper, gifted with both a world class set of pork chop sideburns and the knack evidently for persuading world class legends of country music to appear on his indie label for the love of truck driving music more than for financial rewards.

Here's a partial roll call: Buck Owens, Marty Stuart, Nick Lowe, Red Simpson, Kay Adam's, BR-549, Del Reeves, Junior Brown, Son Volt, Steve Earle, Bill Kirchen and the mighty Don Walser. Good lord, this is the only CD in my rack where you can hear Texas legends Dale Watson and Wayne Hancock on the same track together ("Six days on the road") along with a batch of other well known Texas singers.

This is as star studded a collection as has been assembled since the days of STARDAY records. It's action packed. My favorite tracks: "Truck Driving Man" by Don Walser, "Nitro Express" by Red Simpson and Junior Brown", "White Freightliner Blues" by Steve Earle and "Mama Was a Rock (Daddy Was a Rolling Stone) by Kay Adams with BR-549 and the afore mentioned Austin all stars track "Six Days...".

This CD should serve as a reminder that even though the country charts are mostly loaded with impostors there's an army of real country singers willing to go to bat for the authentic stuff.

"ROAD MUSIC" Compilation (1978) Gusto Records. 2 LP set.

This one's flat out stuffed with high grade truck driving tunes. We're treated to two Dudley classics, a grand total of seven Sovines and a brilliant array of many of the greatest recordings ever from the truckin' genre including: "Pinball Machine" by Lonnie Irving, "C.B.Savage" by Rod Hart and "Passing Zone Blues" by Coleman Wilson.

You've heard of the old "desert island album" picks? I'll nominate this one here and now for the one cassette I'd want in the cab of my rig if I drove a truck for a living and was only allowed one by the Highway Patrol. A full three quarters of these songs can be found spread out amongst various albums in this book. The folks at Gusto really did a helluva job on this one. Look for it in the bargain bin at your local truck stop, it's not hard to find.

ROD HART "Breakeroo!" (1976) Plantation Records. LP.

This album obviously saw the light of day based upon the strength of the leadoff tune, the perfect C.B. radio song "C.B. SAVAGE" which is a hilarious gay exploitation take on the late '70's craze. If there was ever an album I'd buy to hear one song over and over this is it. There's plenty of other strong numbers though such as "Big Fanny," which is a horror story about the ultimate obese, greasy haired gal. It's funny as hell and is guaranteed to piss off your p.c. friends.

"Charlie's Moonshine Bar and Grill" is catchy as hell and worth repeated listens. There are a couple weak spots though such as the slapped together sounding "Gary Grasshopper & Tillie Tadpole" which sounds like a song Barney would sing until the last line, which is too late to save it. And how come there are not one but two, so-so "dog" songs on this album? Chalk it up to producer Shelby Singleton. Mr. Hart didn't write any of the inferior songs and he pops in here and there with his gay shtick often enough to keep a smile on my face. The hand drawn cover is a masterpiece too.

"THAT'S TRUCKDRIVIN'" (1960's) Starday Records. LP.

This is as close to a perfect compilation record as has ever been released. That's saying something since Starday also released a handful of other sampler albums that are almost as good. This album is the best of the bunch in my book. My buddy Jello Biafra turned me on to this one.

I must have 200 vinyl country compilation albums lining my over crowded record shelves. Most of them blend of two or three worthy songs from the label's best artists with a batch of tunes laying around by mediocre preliminary bums.

"That's Truck Drivin'" is so good it seems like the label set out to make the best collection of songs possible as opposed to promoting new artists or spreading the word on average product.

We've got four Red Sovine songs, a quartet of his best: "Giddyup go" plus "Truck Driving Son-of-a-Gun" "Girl on the Billboard" and "A Kiss And the Keys." The Willis Brothers incredibly cool "Convoy in the Sky" is included along with the boot stomping "Long Haul Weekend."

Johnny Bond's several tracks include the topnotch "Hi-way Man" and "Johnny Overload" (which I always sing along to at the top of my lungs). Slim Jacob's "That's Truck Drivin'" is a down-home tale that's the sort of song designed to tickle the funny bone of depressed drivers who've had a miserable go of it on that ol' endless gray ribbon. Joe Maphis "10 Days Out 2 Days In" is another great sing-along number, preferably as you're driving down some lonely interstate.

I consider it a stroke of genius that a couple of fine Tommy Hill string band tracks are included. Many of the other songs are of the wordy story-song variety and it's nice to have an instrumental break once in a while. I usually take the opportunity to stomp on the accelerator and pass a dozen or two vehicles. Fourteen songs, no filler. Just one more reason why the Starday Records label was (and is) a sign of quality.

"THUNDER on the ROAD" Compilation. Starday. LP.

When I first started out combing the thrift stores and flea market record bins of America many years ago, I learned right off an important rule: always pick up any Starday record you see. It's amazing how consistently good the releases on Starday were, perhaps more consistent than even the Sun label. This album is bloated with top drawer tracks by Red Sovine, the Willis Brothers, Johnny Bond and Minnie Pearl. That's right, no filler whatsoever, just these titans of country music. They took time out of their busy schedules to pose with a Nashville cop on the front cover of this disc. These are all songs of the road that (to quote the liner notes) "reflect the excitement and romance of American life."

Side one starts off with the classic title track "Thunder on the Road" by Johnny Bond who chips in with three other tracks including: "Giddyup Hobo" and the odd bittersweet salute to cabbies: "Taxicab Man." Red Sovine is in fine form contributing three songs including the frisky,"Hitch Hiking Girl."

The Willis Brothers as usual aren't about to be left in the dust. Their epic "Diesel Smoke on Danger Road" and their salute to two wheelers: "Motorcycle Bill" are included amongst their four tunes. Only one Minnie Pearl song is used, the album closing answer to Red's "Giddyup Go." Even though I've heard it dozens of times it still brings an iddy biddy tear to my eye.

A mighty assemblage of talent that would stand shoulder to shoulder with a similar compilation by any of the major labels from this period.

WILLIS BROTHERS "24 Great Truck Drivin' Songs" CD.

There's something to be said for loading up on Willis Brothers recordings in multiple formats. Their old Starday label album covers are beautiful works of art that a fella naturally wants to hold in his lap and stare at whilst listening to their catchy, guitar driven, often hilarious takes on adultery, drinking and hauling goods. On the other hand it's hard to top the convenience of popping this disc into ye olde CD player for an hour straight of fun. You still have the option to gaze at your album covers simultaneously for that matter.

Believe it or not I own the cassette version of this release too since it only cost me $2.99 at a truck stop in West Virginia. It's proven to be a damned popular item in our car during long road trips. My kid prefers the Willis Brothers to many of the more subtle, introspective country legends. Hell, I can't blame him. They're without a doubt funnier than a triple trailer load of rubber crutches. The world would certainly be a better place if kids everywhere listened to the Willis Brothers for just one month instead of all that hip-hop hogwash.

It's hard not to stomp the accelerator to the floor listening to songs like "Give Me 40 Acres" "Blazing Smokestack" and "Long Haul Weekend." The funnier songs are a perfect antidote for road rage "Diesel Drivin' Donut Dunkin' Dan" "Alcohol and #2 Diesel" for example. The Brothers also had a real knack for slightly slower spooky numbers such as "Diesel Smoke on Thunder Road" that chill your blood and keep you on the edge of your seat.

Nope, you can't go wrong with the Willis Brothers. You may consider piping them into your bathroom like I have, or substituting them for door chimes. Your family will sure as hell take notice if you get off your duff and print up some color photocopies down at your local Kinko's of their old album covers to serve as wallpaper. How's about canceling your overpriced cable TV service and converting your homes televisions into 24 hour a day Willis Brothers video monitors? Next you can insert some more wallet sized pic's of the Brothers into your family album and cut out cardboard stencils so you can spray paint "Willis" and "Brothers" down the full length of your left and right pants legs.

WILLIS BROTHERS "Give Me 40 Acres" (mid-1960's) Starday. LP.

In retrospect Starday and the Willis boys teamed up to create some of the finest works of art from the mid-1960's including both the beautiful colorful album covers and the consistently good music on the platters themselves. The difference between thumbing through a stack of Willis Brothers Starday LPs and a pile of major label albums or contemporary CDs by almost anybody else is stunning.

It's like the difference between bunking overnight at a classic neon garnished motel with a Tiki theme or perhaps at one of those elaborate facilities where each room is an Indian teepee, compared to the humdrum, run of the mill, box shaped chain motel room of today.

Just as listening to a collection of old Carter family songs will educate you to the ways and traditions of mountain folk, spinning a Willis Brothers album or two can update you on the lifestyle and habits of the great American truck driver of the 1950's-60's.

From this album alone we hear songs about him pushing his rig down the road on a good day in America like "Blazing Smoke Stack" and "Truck Driving Sam" songs about his gal's such as "Truck stop Cutie" and the salty, suggestive "Too Early to Get Up."

Songs to make him laugh like "Give Me 40 Acres." The lyrics use a lot of trucker lingo, making Willis Brothers albums the next best thing to being allowed to sit in the driver section of the truck stop coffee shop.

My son and a few of my friends who prefer rock and roll to country music likewise prefer the Willis boys to 95% of the rest of what you're reading about in this book. They are drawn to the bodacious twangy guitar work, the catchy harmonies and the overall good natured, never overly serious feel of the songs.

The WILLIS BROTHERS "Road Stop Jukebox Hits" Starday Records. LP.

Since the genre's inception early in the 20th century there've always been a lot of two man brother acts performing country music. The three Willis Brothers: Guy, Skeeter and Vic out sang and out picked 'em all from the Osbornes to the Everlys to the Louvins in the same manner that Pro-Wrestling's first three man "brother" tag team "the Fabulous Freebirds," out manned the plethora of two man teams.

It couldn't be just coincidence that literally any Starday LP by the boys is entertaining from beginning to end. It must have something to do with superior genetics. There's less filler on this album than even most of the finest albums in this book. They were just flat out that good. Their songs were almost all catchy, up-tempo and totally devoted first and foremost (as they should be) to entertaining our nation's mighty knights of the road.

Side one of this LP starts with "Pinball Anonymous" the best pinball oriented song ever. "Credit Card" and "Six Foot 2 X 4" are both hilarious songs that could make a lonely trucker smile thinking about the little lady back home. “Love Thy Neighbor” is a bit saucy as is “Gonna Swing Til My Rope Breaks.” As usual for the Willis boys this album is of special interest to fans of cool reverb guitar.

14. TUNE WARBLERS

CLAUDE GRAY "The Easy Way of" (1967) Decca. LP.

Hey, Claude Gray has everything going for him. He's got an easy going bass voice almost as deep as Dick Curless's. On the cover of this LP he's wearing a flashy red suit and he's from Texas to boot. His choice of familiar cover tunes is great: "Nightlife" "Crazy Arms" "Little Old Wine Drinker Me" and a fine rendition of Dean Martin's hit "Houston."

His tunes that aren't familiar hits for somebody else such as "If I Ever Need a Lady" and "Your Devil Memory" are well chosen and showcase Claude's voice well. He's not quite the consummate crooner as the illustrious, world class Dean Martin, but he sings with more sincere country charm and sincerity than Dino did on many of his country western recordings.

The backing band is a good old meat and potatoes six-piece combo plus strings and elaborate orchestrations are kept to a minimum. As was common for this day and age though, there is a gaggle of background vocals present that resemble the Anita Kerr singers. Backing vocals like this are totally out of place accompanying a helluva lot of singers on loads of records made in the '60's. In this case, they seem to compliment Gray's vocals in the same way that they never seemed to interfere with Porter Wagoner or Roy Orbison or many other singers. This LP isn't meant for barn dances. It's a great choice for quietly sippin' your first few bourbon and waters of the evening to.

DEAN "Tex" MARTIN "Country Style" (1963) Reprise Records. LP.

I've got to admit it's a bit of a stretch to expect a multi-millionaire Hollywood celebrity to deliver a respectful country album, but think how many singers honored with a spot in this book appear to be influenced heavily by ol' Dino?

From Jim Reeves to Jim Ed Brown to Elvis himself, every country crooner and every session producer had to have been listening to Dean Martin along with the rest of the world. He wasn't just another singer he was a unique musical institution. Whereas guys like Sinatra and Bennett had fine sets of pipes too they didn't have the rugged, virile charm or the "don't give a shit" coolness that Dean exuded.

Just think how well Martin fit in next to John Wayne on screen in "Son's of Katie Elder". He was a man's man and he deserves to be treated respectfully by country music fans despite the fact that he didn't have the country roots of Ernest or Lefty .

Some of these songs work pretty well such as Dean's takes of "Singing The Blues" and "Things." His two Hank songs "I'm So Lonesome I Could Cry" and "Hey Good Lookin'" are respectful and decent. Hell, it's fun to hear how such an icon from a different way of life handles a Hank song. I draw the line at the skirt chasing Dean's reading of "I Walk the Line". I simply can't take that one seriously. Still, Johnny Cash kindly returned the favor with a '90's cover of Dean's old hit "Memories Are Made of This" that really hit the spot but that's another story.

Incidentally, I saw an ad for a Dean Martin "country" CD including these songs in my Sunday paper just last week proving that they've clearly stood the test of time.

FRANKIE LAINE "Hell Bent for Leather" (1960) Columbia Records. LP.

Where is it etched in stone that western music need be slowly strummed on an acoustic guitar in a somber manner? Frankie's up-tempo take on the genre is exciting, exhilarating and makes me want to tip a fifth of rye whiskey or something.

This album features some classic recordings no doubt. "Mule Train" is one of my favorite songs period. The catchy theme from TV's "Rawhide" has been covered by everybody from the Blues Brothers to the Dead Kennedys (both versions are jolly toe tappers). It's just a great song that would be hard to screw up like "Cocaine Blues" for instance. "High Noon" "Bowie Knife" hell this album belongs to that select group of those which can be played from the first track to the last without ever hitting a boring spot.

The electric guitar playing on this album is quite decent the drumming and percussion innovative. The layered soundtrack style backup vocals are an asset in my book, as opposed to being excess baggage like you could argue about many an album from this time period.

MARVIN RAINWATER "Songs By" (1957) MGM Records. LP.

An album loaded with primo tunes by a guy who should be much better known. The material here ranges from songs that loosely fit the Hank Sr. mold such as "Where Do We Go From Here" and "What Am I Supposed To Do?" to some insanely unique novelty and rockabilly numbers.

The Hank-like numbers are so Hank-like musically speaking that they have me suspecting that some of his ex band mates played on those tracks, this is Hank's old record label after all. "Tennessee Hound Dog Yodel" is a bizarre blast that will have your house pets running for cover. I'm amazed the Cramps never recorded it. "Get off the Stool" is funny but "Tea Bag Romeo" is so crazy in a '50's hipster way that I'm not even sure what it's about.

My favorite track is "Gonna Find Me a Bluebird" which features some melancholy whistling '50's country style. I'm as much a sucker for whistling on records as I am for those singing fish you nail to your wall.

"PAINT YOUR WAGON" Soundtrack Paramount Records. LP.

A lot of this album represents what it best about the Western half of the Country & Western genre marriage. The film plot itself is centered around a theme at the heart of many great country songs, the age old fork in the road where you have to choose between seeking wealth and gold versus the simple life.

The greatest song to be heard here is Lee Marvin's harsh but beautiful bass voice singing a rover's anthem: "I Was Born Under a Wandering Star." I can't say enough about this great, gargled song. Clint Eastwood does his best with "I Talk To the Trees" and in a great Hollywood aural moment duets nicely with gravel voiced Lee ("Best Things").

Harve Presnell absolutely booms out "They Call the Wind Maria" backed by a massive and stately Western style orchestral arrangement that's as bracing as a cold skinny dip in a mountain stream. The Nitty Gritty Dirt Band chip in with "Hand Me Down That Can of Beans". Overall, a solid album I'd ride the river with any day.

SLIM WHITMAN "All My Best" Suffolk Marketing. LP.

A lot of albums sold on TV back in the day were poor values upon close inspection. Some of them featured re-recorded versions of hits. A few cheap ass label scallywags even ruthlessly edited songs into much shorter versions than what folks were used to hearing on the radio.

Not so this LP. It's a fantastic value loaded with twenty great Slim Whitman songs. I remember how the ads on TV for Slim Whitman's albums in the late '70's led to jokes by comedians everywhere. The beauty of these songs is no joke however no matter whether they're currently in vogue or not.

"Indian Love Call" leads off with a warbled blend of yodeling and steel guitar riffs that really tickles my fancy. "My Happiness" and "I Love You Because" obviously inspired the very young Sun label era Elvis Presley to a great extent. Slims version of "Blue Eyes Cryin' in the Rain" is the prettiest I've ever heard. There are no honky tonkin' drinking tunes to be heard here and for once I don't care. This album is the musical equivalent of binging on sweet, sweet fudge.

.

15. WEST COAST

BUCK OWENS "Carnegie Hall Concert" (1966) Capitol. LP.

At the time of this live concert in NYC in 1966, Buck and his boys had been on top of the country music charts for a good while. Of course that irked sour pusses in Nashville like bitter ol' Roy Acuff who probably expected Buck to kiss up to him and his cronies and appear at the Ryman on a weekly basis for peanuts. Buck said no thank you and went on to conquer the country charts from his west coast base of operations inspiring many others who followed in his wake

It must have galled the Opry gang even more when Buck lit up the big apple all on his own with this stunning show instead of holding back and doing it as part of a Nashville approved package show. The set opens with a song the urban crowd was familiar with thanks to the Beatles "Act Naturally." There are a few other songs sung in their entirety "Love's Gonna Live Here Again" "Tiger By the Tail" and several medleys to work all of the other familiar songs in. The Buckaroo's Don Rich, Tom Brumley, Doyle Holly and

Willie Cantu are in top form and this album cruises along without let up.

In many cases especially back in the '60's a live album meant inferior versions of hits with poor sound quality; that's definitely not the case here. Buck Owens wasn't about to screw up this big chance to swagger a bit in the limelight as country's top dog of the decade.

BUCK OWENS "I've Got a Tiger by the Tail" (1964) Capitol. LP.

A lot of LP back-cover liner notes make all sorts of outrageous and unsubstantiated claims about the chart and career success of the featured artist. Not so this album. Case in point; we are informed on the back cover of this classic 1964 platter that Buck has "the world by the tail on a downhill pull." That's no exaggeration.

Buck kicked ass throughout the 1960's while remaining based out of Bakersfield. The west coast had enjoyed many, many years of tip-top country music by the time the '60's came around but a lot of it was imported from Texas and Tennessee and elsewhere. Buck's success proved that a country artist didn't necessarily have to march to the tune of the powers that be in Nashville years before the "outlaw" movement came to be recognized.

Furthermore, Buck's heavy use of twangy fender electric guitars, electric bass and a drum kit and the fact that the Beatles were influenced big time by his work is proof positive that if he didn't personally invent country-rock, he sure as goddamned hell had been recording it for years before the falsely touted great pretender innovators of country rock Gram Parsons and his ilk.

So why does Buck never receive proper credit for his rocking up country music? (along with Waylon and many others in the early '60's) Just maybe because Buck didn't shoot dope with Rolling Stone magazine reporters or influential rock band musicians like Keith from the Stones. A great deal is made of the fact that Mr. Parson's band wore Nudie suits whilst playing their "country rock". Guess what Buck is wearing on the cover of this and many other of his albums that precede the founding of the Byrds, the Burrito's, etc.?

This album is crammed with great songs. First off we've got a title track that is arguably one of the best twenty songs or so of all time. "Cryin' Time" is one of the best weepers of the 1960's decade. "Fallin' For You" and "We're Gonna Let the Good Times Roll" are just two of the great up tempo numbers that feature high class west coast style picking.

Merle Haggard and other California talents would've made it anyway without Buck blazing a path, but they all would've sounded different more like standard Nashville artists. All you fab four fans speculate for a moment how different your lovable mop tops would have sounded during this phase of their career without Buck's guitar driven sound to influence 'em. HHmmm?

DWIGHT YOAKAM "Guitars Cadillacs etc.etc." (1986) Warner Bros. LP.

Popping up out of nowhere in the mid 80's was young Dwight Yoakam with a topnotch, real country album. This was approximately at the same time in which many veteran country legends were being rewarded for their years of quality music with pink slips by a new breed of suits in Nashville bent on replacing them with young jock-hunks and gals that looked like flawless models.

Yoakam sure as hell wasn't part of the problem though, you simply can't lump him in with all the stud-country goofballs. He convincingly breathes new life and youthful zest into classics like Harlan Howard's "Heartaches By the Number" "Ring of Fire" and Johnny Horton's "Honky Tonk Man."

His solid original compositions really put this album over the top though including the toe tapping title track and a great ode to the bottle "It Won't Hurt." To my understanding Dwight avoided the mistake of many young country artists by refusing to allow the biz to burn him out by overbooking him so as to squeeze every penny possible out of him. Bully for him. Things would sure as hell be different today if the industry had managed to find fifteen or twenty more authentic guys like Yoakam back when he hit the top of the charts.

The MADDOX BROTHERS & ROSE Vol.1 Arhoolie. CD

The subtitle to this release is "America's most colorful hillbilly band". Well, I don't know about that. I think it's plain that they earned bragging rights when it came to west coast family hillbilly acts for many years. This CD features a whopping twenty-seven tracks originally released during the years 1946-1951. Unlike a lot of lengthy reissue collections this one never lets up.

It starts out with a toe tappin' band introduction song with a galloping beat titled "Georges Playhouse Boogie." A couple tracks later the band kicks into the next gear with the hot "Shimmy Shakin' Daddy" which predates the supposed birth of rockabilly by a few years. Then there's the "New Step It Up and Go" which plainly rocks more than it boogie-woogies.

There's even a wild guitar lead with showoff riffs accompanied by the band bellowing in the background. The capper of the fast songs on this collection is the electric guitar driven instrumental "Water Baby Boogie" that simply kicks butt. I'd like to see a dance floor full of people dancing to a song that rip snortin.'

Yes folks the country music sub-genre later named rockabilly was alive and well out on the west coast years before Elvis even graduated from high school.

This CD features a mixture of songs of varying styles and speeds and it isn't all hopped up juke joint boogie. Sister Rose is the main voice of the band and she does a helluva job leaving her own mark on familiar often covered songs like "Honky Tonkin'" and "Mule Train." Her voice isn't up-town, it's relaxed and homespun.

To handle bleak Carter family style songs such as "Careless Driver" and "Dark As a Dungeon" she blends her voice with her brothers respectfully. The Maddox family as a whole sounds respectfully traditional and southern on the slow tunes; they seem to be more innovative on the fast songs. I can't imagine the Stoneman's or Carter's or other Appalachian family bands tearing it up like this clan. For that matter, A.P. Carter probably would've had a stroke if he heard the Maddox's cuttin' loose with their salty tunes "Whoa Sailor" and "Meanest Man in Town" which is a ballad celebrating the wicked ways of a mangy womanizer.

By all accounts the meetings between Jimmie Rodgers and the Carter's for recording purposes were cordial at best (I read that he tried unsuccessfully to pitch woo to Maybelle). Jimmie was a wildcat and a stud; no matter how beautiful the Carter's music he must have been bored stiff watching 'em drink iced tea and shovel in potato salad or knit or whittle for kicks. I bet he would've found some kindred spirits in the Maddox family if he could've been transported, by some sort of sci-fi time travel gadget. I can picture him passing the jug with them and maybe later struttin' his stuff tom-cat wise in Rose's direction.

MERLE HAGGARD "A Working Man Can't Get Nowhere Today" (1977) LP.

Three masterpiece Haggard songs included here. First we've got the title song which is illustrated by the cover picture of Merle sitting on a bus stop bench with a lunch pail, a strange hard-hat that appears to be several sizes too small and a smoke hanging out of his mouth. "Working Man.." is a blue collar anthem that only a boss would hate. "Goodbye Lefty" is a heartfelt loving tribute to Lefty Frizell that is worth the price of the album alone. "I'm a White Boy" has probably too politically incorrect a title to stand a chance of airplay by today's putrid happy-face "country" stations. There's nothing even remotely racist about this song, it's simply another great blue collar anthem released in the same decade a jillion "black is beautiful" type songs made the airwaves. Merle is white; he'd seem pretty weird singing about being a proud black man now wouldn't he?

The cover version of Hank's "Moanin' the Blues" and the Merle penned "Running Kind" stand out and will have you beating a tattoo with your knuckles on your lunch pail. Hey, I got tuna fish sandwiches today. I'll swap you for your bologna?

MERLE HAGGARD "Back to the Barrooms" (1980) MCA Records. LP.

A classic concept album loaded with songs spanning the painful kiss off by a significant other on through to the first glimmers of hope that a new love can be found. The album leads off in a mood of despair with "Misery and Gin" and the title track "Back To the Barrooms Again" to set the general mood. "Make-up and Faded Blue Jeans" warns against running straight out to pick up the first available honky tonk vixen you see on the rebound.

"Easy Come Easy Go" and "I Don't Want to Sober Up Tonight" are a bit happier reflecting the transition from the initial sting of being dumped to seeing the positive side of the split. "Our Paths May Never Cross" is a beautiful wistful song about some practical romantic prospects for the future.

"I Don't Have Anymore Love Songs" is nice and feisty and a natural lead in to the last track "I Think I'll Just Stay Here and Drink." The relationship is officially over. It's sung from the standpoint of a guy who has come to grips with the situation enough to recognize the wisdom of filling a barstool and getting plowed rather than mope or try to beg his way back. I recommend gazing at the bleary-eyed cover picture of Merle while listening to this one.

MERLE HAGGARD "Branded Man" (1966) Capitol Records. LP.

A lot of great country songs have been an unexpected benefit of an otherwise horrid situation. For example, how many great songs resulted from the self-destructive lifestyles of Hank Williams Sr. and George Jones to name just two guys who went through hellish bad spells with their Women. No songwriter in their right mind would consider a stretch in prison time well spent no matter how many successful songs they were able to write about the experience. I once played in a rock band with a singer/ lyricist whose personal life was always tragic.

The other folks in the band and I would sympathize to his face whenever one of the rare Women he got close to told him off or dumped him. Behind his back, as cruel as it sounds we'd be high fiving and evilly beaming with joy, sure that he'd get a couple good bitter songs out of his latest sad experience.

Merle Haggard did indeed wind up at San Quentin many years ago, but he didn't need to capitalize on being an alumni of the California State penal system to become an overnight country superstar. He didn't even write "I'm a Lonesome Fugitive". He did write the follow up which is the title song of this album and is every bit as strong. Tommy Collins contributes two numbers here "I Made the Prison Band" and a love letter tune from the viewpoint of a prisoner "Don't Get Married."

Merle further displays his world class writing skills with "I Threw Away the Rose" which leads off side two and later "Some Of Us Never Learn." Capitol Records didn't attempt to exploit Merle's prison record in the liner notes. That was a wise move showing that they recognized his potential was much greater than that of a mere exploitation song bad boy.

MERLE HAGGARD "Same Train a Different Time" (1969) Capitol Records. 2 LP set.

Since Jimmie Rodgers death in 1933, he has gradually faded from recognition by the masses. At the same time he's been remembered and put on a pedestal by a huge number of legendary artists over the years. There've been a helluva lot of loving vinyl tributes over the last several decades from fellow performers ranging from Ernest Tubb, Lefty Frizell and Elton Britt to Hank Snow and Johnny Cash.

This double album includes several narrative passages by Merle to help educate the fans of the day to country music's first major star. It's a tribute to Merle Haggard's generosity and greatness that in the prime of his career he could devote two entire hunks of vinyl to another performer. Today the world badly needs another contemporary reminder of Jimmie Rodgers, but I don't see Nashville's current crop of prettyboy artists paying tribute to anybody who might draw attention away from themselves.

Given the talent level of Merle and his band it's a no-brainer that these songs are great versions. "California Blues" appropriately starts the session off and "Jimmie Rodgers Last Blue yodel (Women Make a Fool Out of Me)" is its bookend wrapping up side four. In between, Merle covers "Peach Picking Time in Georgia" "Mule Skinner Blues" "Waitin' For a Train" and a lot of other old favorites. Merle doesn't pull out any exotic experimental arrangements, but why should he? He's Merle Haggard and the songs are all classics by Jimmie Rodgers. How could this not be a great album?

MERLE HAGGARD "My Farewell to Elvis" (1977) MCA. LP.

A fine salute, from a fellow legend and standup guy. Elvis Presley may have been king of rock and roll, but when he left this planet all too soon he sure as hell left behind a large number of country singers trying to sing country songs his way.

At the beginning of his career when he was singing on country package tours he pissed off a lot of the old-timers who couldn't follow his physical performances. As Elvis fame grew so did rock and roll, while country music simultaneously declined in popularity. That wasn't his fault though. He was just a country boy doing the best he could. And he was never disrespectful towards the great country singers who inspired him as a boy growing up listening to the radio.

Mr. Haggard sings these songs in his own style rather than try to out Elvis-Elvis. "Heartbreak Hotel" has been my favorite track on this LP for the 20 years I've been wearing out my copy with its double tracked eerie vocal effect. "In The Ghetto" sounds so good and fits Merle like a glove. It's plain that if Hag had gotten to the song before Elvis it would've been a hit for him. "Jailhouse Rock" and "Blue Suede Shoes" don't quite match up to Elvis's classic versions even with the Jordanaires singing along, but that's not the point of this album. Like I said it's a loving tribute and one of the top two or three of the mountain of them recorded after Presley's death.

MERLE HAGGARD "Swinging Doors" (1965) Capitol Records. LP.

A great early career Merle LP. Side one starts off with "Swinging Doors" for which Merle would be remembered if his career had gone nowhere after its release. Side two starts off with (according to the album back cover liner notes) a "kind of sequel" to "..Doors" none other than the infamous and often interpreted "Tonight the Bottle Let Me Down".

Not content to simply go through the motions cranking out classic drinking songs, Merle shows a great deal of versatility here. "I Can't Stand Me" is a fine telecaster driven rocked up number that calls Buck Owens and raises him a sawbuck. Merle's "The Girl Turned Ripe" is a brave analogy to say the least for a mid '60's country song. Even though this album is early on in his career he proves that he's not going to be content to merely ape his musical heroes. "Shade tree (Fix-it man)" is a creative and different sort of song which is a sign of even greater things to come as Haggard came of age.

MERLE HAGGARD "The Fightin' Side of Me" (live in Philly) (1970) Capitol Records. LP.

A classic live album, with performances as strong and as timeless as Johnny Cash's prison recordings. This was recorded in Philadelphia around 1970, and starts out with a batch of Merle's hits ("Okie.." "Today I Started Loving You Again" etc.) and a terrific impersonation medley. Next up are a couple instrumental bits by his band the Stranger's and a vocalized number by the great Bonnie Owens.

The back cover shows photos of Merle checking out the Liberty Bell and Independence Hall. As of this writing the familiar landmarks are still there, Merle's still around in California but there's unfortunately no sign of country radio WEEZ which sponsored this concert nor are there any other stations in Philly that broadcast decent traditional country music.

It's a shame, but life goes on. I got to see Merle play live in a large hall 50 miles West of Philadelphia in 2001 in a medium size town. The hall was filled to busting with thousands of folks paying $50 per ticket to see him and Bonnie and his band. I mention to this prove that even though the pop-country music biz jackals have done their best to remove veteran country artists like Merle from the spotlight many people across this nation are still anxious as hell to see him.

Even though the song list at that live show in 2001 was very similar to the songs performed 30 years earlier, on this old familiar record album, it was hardly just a singer going through the motions. There was electricity in the air that gave me goose bumps several times. An evening with Merle Haggard is an event no matter what the year is and no matter whether you're seeing him live or hearing a great masterpiece live album like this one. I owned this album for many years hoping I'd one day have the chance to see a performance like this one live; that's one function of a good live record album like this one.

16. KEEPERS OF THE FLAME

BR5-49 "Big Backyard Beat Show" (1998) Arista Records. CD.

The most remarkable thing about this damn good album is the fact that it was issued in 90's Nashville. How in the hell did these boys slip between the cracks? This disc is everything that commercial country music should be in modern times. It's fun to listen to, based on the traditions of real country music, totally cleansed of typical contemporary over-production and synthesizer free.

This album is a logical continuation of what Buck Owens and his Buckaroos were doing in the 1960's as opposed to being a clone of that sound. Indeed. The album opener is Buck's "There Goes My Love," performed at a medium up-tempo clip with sugar sweet harmonies. Throughout the album tasteful use is made of fiddles, mandolins, steel guitar, etc. to fit the mood of the individual song. "18 Wheels and a Crowbar," is a badass novelty tune played in a style that will please any Dick Curless or Dave Dudley fan.

"Out of habit," and "You Flew the Coop," are two more flawless original numbers on the up-tempo side that make me wish I wasn't a two left foot wallflower. Toss in a couple more high-octane covers; "Wild One" and "Seven Nights to Rock" and this disc is already overflowing with goodness. The grand finale version of Billy Joe Shaver's "Georgia on a Fast Train" ends things off on a high note, like a pinball machine racking up a mountain of bonus points.

Yeah, out of fourteen songs I could honestly do without a couple of the slow ones, but it's a matter of personal taste. Twelve out of fourteen great songs on one album was perhaps the standard many years ago for guys like Hank Thompson and Ernest Tub. It's a miracle in this day and age when I'd feel surprised and lucky to get even one passable song out of an album sanctioned by the biz.

DALE WATSON "Dalevis" CD

A loving tribute, Dale Watson style to the King. Ten songs all recorded at the legendary site of Elvis's first several recording sessions, Sun Studios. Watson doesn't try to "be" Elvis; he's not imitating him in the least or really singing particularly different than you'd hear him sing at a Chickenshit Sunday gig at Ginny's Longhorn Saloon in

Austin. He just lets Presley's natural influence upon him guide him through the songs.

"Blue Moon" and "That's all Right Mama," percolate along nicely with Dale's wistful vocals accompanied by the same instrumentation that Elvis, Scotty and Bill used. "When My Blue Moon Turns to Gold" gives the original a run for its money as does "Big Boss Man" and even "I Was the One" probably based on the fact that Dale is a more seasoned professional than Elvis was when he sang these songs. Dale Watson proves once again that he's one of the absolute best country singers on the planet under the age of 70.

DALE WATSON "Every Song I Write is for You" Audium. CD.

I've written elsewhere in this book about how "fortunate" in a bittersweet way certain songwriters are to find themselves neck deep in personal misfortunes that inspire topnotch songs. This album of songs is to my knowledge unique and matchless in the entire body of country music, but it sure as hell is an album Dale Watson would've just as soon never written. These songs were all written after he lost his soul mate to an auto accident.

This is a very difficult collection of songs to listen to in a casual and ordinary workday state of mind. On the other hand, if I knew of someone suffering from a similar loss I'd get a copy of this to them right away. This isn't an exploitation album. If anything it makes those sorts of albums seem a bit silly and weak. Dale completely bares his soul here but maintains a tone of dignity that elevates this album beyond fictitious crying-in-your-beer tragedy songs.

That's not to say sad or morbid honky-tonk songs designed to get you waving your beer can don't have their place. You won't hear any of those sorts of songs on this CD though.

This isn't a preachy album. Dale sounds like he's still in shock to an extent and not in any shape to focus on our lives. At the point this album was recorded it sounds like he's still got memories and anxieties to deal with and sort out, but he's past the worst.

Besides the title track a few of the especially moving numbers to me are "I'd Deal With the Devil" "I See Your Face in Every Face I See" "Angel in my Dreams" and "These Things we'll Never Do."

In terms of sincere country music artistic expression this album is on a par with Jimmie Rodgers trying to laugh in the face of impending death with his "TB Blues" and Hank Sr. begging with cracking voice "Oh PLEASE...don't make me love you..."

There are positive aspects to this collection of songs taken as a whole that show glimpses of hope and adjustment that Jimmie the kid and Hank weren't around long enough to express. Quite possibly you're bound to view your significant other in a more appreciative light after walking a mile in Dale's shoes.

DALE WATSON & His Lone Stars "The Truckin' Sessions" CD .

In this age of contrived and over produced industry hogwash that doesn't sound country at all, I'm sure that there are quite literally millions of upset traditional country music fans who are convinced the mold has been broken and there will be no more decent country music again. I feel sorry for these folks whom for whatever reason haven't been able to figure out how to find the still satisfying music of guys like Dale Watson.

This CD isn't a rehashing or aping of the great truck driving songs of generations past, it's not nostalgic in any way. Watson has used the music of the masters like Dave Dudley and Red Simpson and Del Reeves as a starting point.

All fourteen tracks are original songs that celebrate the lifestyle of the knights of the road, and Dale himself writes All of them. To be completely honest, quality wise the songs on this CD are stronger overall than average studio albums by even the mightiest legends that specialized in trucker tunes. Go back and listen closer to those albums. You'll often find three or four songs you usually skip around in favor of the best tunes. Dale is as good a songwriter as he is a performer. You can play this disc straight through.

My favorites are the opening anthem "Good luck 'n Good Truckin' Tonite" the hilarious "Flat Tire" and the philosophical, "Loose Nut Behind the Wheel."

"Exit 109" is catchy as hell with a galloping, twangy guitar and distinctive snare drum rim shots. The final tune is appropriately about getting home at the end of a truck run "I Gotta Get Home to my Baby."

And so ends an album of truck driving songs that prove that the mold hasn't been broken. Traditional country music is not dead. It's just a little bit harder to find than it used to be in some places (luckily, as a Texan by choice I don't live in one of those places).

DALE WATSON "Carryin' On" (2010) E1 Music. CD

I've seen Dale live over twenty times or so down here in Texas. My wife and I have taken friends and relatives to see him and his Lonestars. I even managed to make a Dale fan for life of a discriminating pal from out of state who hates almost everything music wise recorded after 1963.

When he plays multiple sets in one night (which is normal down here at places like the Continental Club and Ginny's Little Longhorn) he masterfully mixes up the speed and mood of the songs. As much as I enjoy hearing truckin' songs and honkytonk rowdy anthems some slower, romantic, or relationship, songs are needed both to keep things from becoming repetitive and to allow folks to hit the dance floor for a few slow dances.

If you're a wallflower or a loser who never scores you might not understand that, but this is the eternal truth since the advent of dancehalls. Guys and gals who are schooled in the ways of romance know you've got to have some songs that allow you to pitch some woo.

Mr. Watson has been packaging theme albums for many years now, a few of which you can read about in the book. This disc is one of them, featuring mid tempo and ballad relationship numbers. I'd venture to say most nostalgic classic country radio station wouldn't hear a complaint if they played songs from it.

Part of the reason it sounds so like the great country of that period is due to the players in the studio, the icons Lloyd Green, Pig Robbins and Pete Wade, all of whom have played on countless recordings covered in this book.

Then there's Dale's masterful song writing. He's a superhero level crafter of clever, memorable words that make for tunes ordinary people can relate to. You'd think he has a telescope peering into his neighbors master bedrooms taking notes of the dialogue and tiny details. Some top notch selections are "For a Little While" "Heart of Stone" and another version of one of his best songs from a few years back "Your Love I'm Gonna Miss."

"Hey Brown Bottle" is a calm drinking song about one of those nights you maintain control. "Carryin' on This Way," is a bittersweet feeling your age number, which is a familiar experience for most of us on the bad side of 40. "Hello, I'm An Old Country Song" is a well-chosen way to end the album that analogizes how country songs effect us in various ways in this life.

HAMMERLOCK "American Asshole" (1996) Man's Ruin. CD.

If this band lived in Texas they'd be playing venues like the Continental Club in Austin to a country audience. Unfortunately, they're horribly mislocated in the bay area, a region that sneers at country music. They're stubborn as hell though, and manage to play at punk rock clubs, biker rallies and private parties fairly often. Some purists might raise an eyebrow at the fact that this was released on a punk rock label, but what the hell that's just one more thing they have in common with fellow Californian Merle Haggard. They also love to fish, stockpile guns and drink Coors beer.

Their music on this particular disc is damned loud and guitar oriented compared to the dreck you'll hear on mainstream biz dominated radio, but lead singer Travis (backed by his bass player wife Liza) sings with authentic country soul. They play a bang-up version of Hag's "Big City" on this disc. They also tackle Tompall Glaser's "Put Another Log on the Fire" and perform the best cover version most likely ever of "He Stopped Loving Her Today."

This isn't what used to be referred to as "cow punk" by a long shot; cow punk bands would take slow ballads and play 'em super fast. Hammerlock takes a slow George Jones song and keeps the tempo the same, but cranks up the intensity. Some of the original songs on this CD are classics that will likely be covered by other bands some day. My favorite is the anti junkie anthem “Sunshine.”

Incidentally, at first I almost felt I should disqualify Hammerlock from this book because I have met these folks and know them well. It always irks me when journalists give their pals rave reviews. In this case we’re dealing with a band that deserves plenty of hype in exchange for years of trying to almost single handedly educate trendy club rats of the Bay Area about country music.

HANK III “Damn Right Rebel Proud” (2008) Sidewalk Records. CD.

The Nashville music industry pop suck ups seem to me to be a gaggle of desperate fucks who will do anything, wear anything, spout any line of bull to “succeed.” Hank III is the very antithesis of this sort of mindset; he’s clearly set out to develop his own fan base. The fact that this inclination seems to run in the family can’t hurt. “The Grand Ole Opry (ain’t so grand)” opens up this batch of tunes waving the flag for real country fans, letting them know this album is gonna be the real McCoy.

The rest of the album is topped off with numbers that aim to resonate with strong individuals ranging from Joe six-pack of today (“Working Man”) to party patrol types (“Me & My Friends” and “Six Pack of Beer”) progressing to a huge salute to the ultimate reprobate of rock GG Allin "P.F.F." In case you thought Mr. III was joshing about GG's spirit, he sings the song twice at two speeds back to back.

"3 Shades of Black" is an anthem that lyrically draws quite a few of his varied fans together under the tent shall we say. It's true folks; you see an impressive array of different sorts of fans at Hank III's shows. I read a boast of his somewhere claiming age wise they span 14-80 and he seems to be on firm ground there. I've personally seen plenty of punk rock types, old farts, modern day pseudo hippies, hotrod rockabilly freaks and even a few outnumbered frat boys at his Texas appearances. He hasn't had to suck ass, cover up the tattoos or totally eliminate his foul language to build an audience.

I betcha some of the country pop suckups I referred to earlier are jealous as shit.

HANK III "Straight to Hell" (2006) Bruc Records. 2 CD's.

Heh heh. That's "Curb" records spelled backwards. This doublewide release isn't just an album, it's an extravaganza akin to an expanded pay per view wrasslin' production.

For your money, besides a mere heap of songs, you get storylines, a variety of moods both familiar and unexpected, guest characters, a few history lessons here and there and a look towards the future.

I can only speculate in my mind as to how many times Hank III has been pinky wagged by squares certain he's hell bound. It's a great angle for an event like this. The art insert features antiquated photos, devilish images and blurbs of info here and there, capped off by a drawn centerfold of III eating a double barrel loaded shotgun to avoid having to hear some of the contemporary pop dreck spewed out by Nashville these days.

The first disc kicks off with a bit of the old Louvin's Sunday school style warning; "Satan is Real" which morph's into a "Straight to Hell" medley. "Thrown out of the Bar," maintains a "don't-give-a-fuck" jolly mood that is infectious. "Country Heroes" is a tribute and demonstration how to hang out with the country icons at your own pad. "D. Ray White" salutes (or introduces the ignorant) to Jesco White's (The Dancing Outlaw) clan.

"Pills I Took" is delivered deadpan, an ode to the bad scenes that we substance users sometimes experience when coming out of the fog. "Smoke & Wine," and "My Drinkin' Problem," are universal sort of honky-tonk anthems and set us up for a brace of self reference numbers that lay down the rowdy Hank III manifesto shall we say: "Crazed Country Rebel," "Dick in Dixie," leaving us a bit winded with the subdued but assured "Not Everybody Likes Us" and the disc ending, classy "Angel of Sin".

Disc two is packed with good stuff you have to take your time to experience; track markers are not to be found. Grab a fifth or a bong and start getting froggy with it. "Louisiana Stripes" is a ballad of prison despair not unlike something Johnny Cash used to deliver.

We enter an abstract vortex point in which sounds including a train, distorted voices and even a frigging answering machine are heard. Along the ensuing way we are treated to a couple of real cover song gems I'll let you discover for your self. This disc will have your ass probably riveted to your chair or perhaps hugging the floor. I'm not positive of the titles of all these tunes, but a couple are incredibly stark and bleak. A well handled, mood swingin' contrast to the tavern friendly GG Allin loving songs from earlier. Yes, the states of Hank III's mind are many and varied on this epic. I bet his label shit bricks over the entire concept. Fuck 'em...

JUNIOR BROWN "Semi Crazy" (1996) Curb Records. CD.

He's multi-talented, versatile, creative and unique, what more can you ask of any entertainer. Junior can pick his custom double neck guitar like mad or use the slide half for just the right aesthetic effect. At will he can launch into a Jimi Hendrix tune, or like on this CD he can whip out a surf medley. He can sing in a booming Dave Dudley manner like on "I Hung it up" or slow it down and sing mellow and sweet like ol' Claude Gray for a slow number "Darlin' I'll do anything you say."

He writes most of his songs. Some of which display his fine sense of humor such as "Joe the Singing Janitor." Hell, he can even cut a damned convincing ice tea commercial. In a perfect world Junior Brown would be as big as Babe Ruth. Instead we live in a world dominated by rap-crap, a genre in which the biggest stars can't play a lick on an instrument or carry a tune in a bucket. What the hell, Junior's music is as great a way to drown out all the worthless fad oriented garbage played on top-40 stations as you're gonna hear. He also dresses a damned sight cooler than all those droopy pants jackasses wearing $250 sneakers I wouldn't wear to scuba dive in a cesspool.

JUNIOR BROWN "Down Home Chrome" (2004) Telarc. CD.

Another fine Junior offering. "Little Rivi-Airhead," kicks things off with a jolly hotrod gal number. "Where Has All the Money Gone" has him chuckling over how his gal is spending him dry. He hits a fast swing tempo and whips out some great guitar licks on "Hill Country Hot Rod Man."

Slowin' things down again he croons an old fashioned sugar sweet duet with his gal (I think) laced with Sunday afternoon steel licks. Grandma would smile at this one. Granny might frown a bit at the bittersweet lovers quarrel tune "Are You Just Cuttin' Up?" Either way, if she digs blistering '60's rock guitar riffs she'll start cutting a rug during Mr. Brown's amazing seven minute Jimi Hendrix cover "Foxy Lady."

The disc wraps up with "Monkey Wrench Blues" a ten minute saga with "kiss off baby" lyrics and a goodly amount of jaw dropping picking punctuated by a couple soulful horns. He preaches how it ain't right for a gal to monkey with a man's automobile. Junior has a wide range of talents and once again he lays out a buffet of sounds.

WAYNE HANCOCK "A-Town Blues" (2001) Bloodshot Records. CD.

His fourth album: this one proves in case anyone's still not convinced, Wayne Hancock is one of a tiny handful of guys working the honky-tonks today who is in the same league with country legends of the past like Ernest Tubb and Webb Pierce. What more can you ask for?

He's got a voice that's a miracle, he writes songs that all those old boys are probably sitting around singing in that saloon in the sky. Even though he clearly digs music from the past, Wayne's as original as anybody, blending together various styles just like the great one Bob Wills. Top it all off with a knack for bringing together brilliant musicians to perfect his songs like steel King Jeremy Wakefield and incredible guitar picker Paul Skelton on this release. Country is not a dead style of music. All the great songs haven't been written. You can hear many damned good new ones on this CD.

The title track and the song that follows it "Man of the Road," both remind us that "Wayne the train" lives out of motels driving an insane number of miles every year to bring us fans all over the country his music. This is his lot in life and he draws pride from it rather than bitch or complain.

"Miller Jack & Mad Dog" is a scary tale of a tragic auto accident. Whenever I see him sing this live I look around to see if any glassy eyed drinkers toss their beers and switch to coffee. Who else besides Wayne, who is plugged into a variety of sounds from the first half of the 20th-century, could pull off the ancient "Viper"?

His version of Jimmie Rodgers "California Blues" is brilliant. Wayne outrageously sustains a note in the chorus seemingly forever and yodels like mad. He humbly introduces the final track "Railroad Blues" as being "Just for the Hell of it." Huh. It's a raw, joyous and instantly memorable classic that merely proves once again that he can tap into the eerie lonesome spirit of ol' Hank's music better than anyone else alive.

WAYNE HANCOCK "That's What Daddy Wants," (1997) Ark 21. CD.

If Wayne had wanted to he undoubtedly could have submitted to a Nashville makeover, and become a big commercial star. It's obvious that he loves country music, real country music as opposed to the impostor commercial hogwash too much to have taken that route.

He also could've chosen a Hank Williams Sr. imitator direction and milked that for some easy money. Instead Wayne Hancock is WAYNE HANCOCK on whatever stage he appears on any given night. If he chooses to sing a Hank tune it's a treat for the audience instead of a case of simply milking Hank's corpse for a buck. His music isn't country poured straight into a glass; it's mixed with blasts of rockabilly and swing and the purity of vision of a man who I'd guess has spent a lot of time on his back porch playing alone to the crickets.

The title track is laden with horns and damned infectious. The bugle call type lick is the perfect way to open an album. The very next song "87 Southbound" has Wayne trudging off down a blazing hot Texas highway with his suitcase after catching his baby fornicatin'. He's such a fine song writer and convincing singer I have no idea whether this actually happened at one point in his life. Let's hope not.

"Highway 54" is a tragic tale wherein two cheaters meet their fate in a collision with a freight train. It's not only a strong candidate for his best song ever, I can say with certainty 99% of the country singers in this book who've left this world, the best of the best would climb up on their chair and yell: "hell yeah Wayne!" if they could hear him. It's sheer proof that it can be done in this day and age.

Topnotch country music for the ages can still be recorded. As hard as the music industry has tried, they still haven't been able to stamp out the real McCoy. In spite of the fact that many "informed" record guides and magazines sometimes erroneously label Wayne as "alternative" country, don't you be fooled for a minute; HE'S the mainstream along with a small handful of others.

The industry with their pop crossover formula's and scheme's is the fashionable "alternative" that will eventually be dumped when they've squeezed the last buck out of it.

WAYNE HANCOCK "Thunderstorms and Neon Signs" 1995. CD.

The debut album by Wayne "the train". The beautiful title track is easily the best expression in recording history of that hard to explain yearning a lot of us have for the road signs, cafes and motels dating back to the heyday of forgotten old highways like Route 66.

While searching the net for a motel in Kingman, Arizona for a recent trip, I learned that Wayne's feelings are shared by sizable numbers of folks from Germany and other European countries who travel halfway around the globe to hunker down in 60 year-old motel rooms most Americans barely glance at as they rush by in their SUV's.

I read a glowing review by a European fellow who was overjoyed to stay at the "Ramblin' Rose" motel thanks to it's perfect view of the railroad tracks. I booked a room there for an upcoming trip as fast as my fingers could punch the keyboard buttons. The fella was right; I could sit on my motel bed nursing a bottle while watching trains roll by every few minutes.

Another one of my favorite numbers from this album is "Cold lonesome Wind," which is one of the world's great homesickness songs. You sure can't beat the foot stompers included either: "Juke Joint Jumpin", "Double A Daddy" and "Friday and Saturday Night."

I think Wayne Hancock's albums are all so uniformly good that they each are considered "the best" by a portion of his loyal fans. As far as my personal opinion, I think this one is a quarter star or so behind the rest. Since it was his first effort you would expect more involvement by other people behind the scenes and I think that shows a tad bit if you listen very closely and compare it to later recordings.

Hancock's greatest talent, even beyond his world class King of the juke joint voice is his vision, which he certainly has put to good use on all his albums. This vision seems to keep getting clearer and clearer as the years go by. That's damn good for us fans who can't wait for his next CD to come out. Bottom line: one of the most tip-top solid debut albums ever.

WAYNE HANCOCK "Tulsa" (2006) Bloodshot Records.

It's hard for even the greatest talents to keep topping themselves. I'm glad Wayne is having a nice career so far, and appears to be oriented towards staying out on the road for many years to come. He stands for quality and has never let the listener down with any of his growing list of full-length releases. I have confidence in him, yet he's hit certain heights that I have to wonder if he can find a way in which to out do himself.

The opening bars of the title track to the earlier reviewed "That's What Daddy Wants" is one of the best kick starts to any album in this book. When I first slapped this disc into my player, goose flesh adorned my arms. Damnit if the opening number "Tulsa" isn't just as catchy. A doghouse bass slaps along under swirling clarinet and trombone. Wayne begins singing the charms of a city ordinarily scorned by all us Texans. When the chorus comes around the band starts calling out the letters "T-U-L-S-A" as Wayne delivers the straight skinny on the pretty women and singular wonders of the town. This one hopefully sent the Tulsa chamber of commerce into action to secure the use of it to attract tourists.

"Drinkin' Blues" reminds us that if Wayne hadn't figured out a way to kick the bottle, he probably wouldn't have made it this far into his career. We wouldn't have him and would be stuck listening to country-rap. "Shootin' Star from Texas" reminds any listeners who got upset at the possibility of Wayne switching allegiance to Oklahoma that he lives on the highway most of the time but reports back to Texas when he needs a rest.

Hancock dials up his depression era voice and belts out "Ain't Gonna Worry No More" over a nice gurgling clarinet and soulful trombone. Beautiful. Next, he stomps on the accelerator with the high octane "Gonna Be Flyin' Tonight." If you dance through all the fine solos you and your partner are gonna need a damn rest. Take five and listen a spell to one of the best hooks on the disc "No Sleep Blues."

Sadly, Wayne gets no sleep and winds up walkin' down to the tracks. "Lord Take My Pain" is a classic honky-tonk "been dumped" weeper you'll dig. "Back Home" finds our vocal protagonist walking down a road in a horrible muggy rainstorm. Memories of home keep him going. Theme wise, you could say this harkens back to the era of Jimmie Rodgers and a million other guys wandering the byways and riding in freight cars. Again though, it's all Wayne. I'm sure he's worn out his share of shoe leather.

The classy, top drawer band all bust out in happy solos during "Goin' to Texas When I'm Through". He's back home from the road for now. If he passes near your neck of the woods next time out, better go catch his show and buy a handful of CDs. There's a couple I haven't had a chance to write about in this book, but they're the real goods too.

WAYNE HANCOCK "Wild Free & Reckless" (1999) Ark 21. CD

If dead folks can perceive what's going on here on earth I can guarantee you that Webb and Ernest and ol' Hank Sr. are clapping their hands to this one. Why? Aren't there a jillion "retro" country acts that pay lip service to them? Didn't all those old hippie soft rock acts like Poco and the whiney Eagles carry on their great music? Haven't the new "jock" country crossover folks paid suitable homage to the music of the big boys of days gone by?

Hell no. With a few exceptions, the singers who proclaim their respect for the forefathers the loudest seem to make the worst music. Let's get real. Hank would've hated California "country rock." Webb would've thought most alternative country acts were talentless bozos. Ernest would've likely flattened any jackass producer who tried to mix drum samples onto one of his songs.

Just like you can't create a true cheese steak outside of Philly you can't create real juke joint boogie-woogie/ honky-tonk music in the spirit of the icons from 50 years ago unless you are sincerely inspired by the essence of the music rather than the desire to make a buck. That's where Wayne Hancock comes in. He doesn't just talk about the legends of country music; he carries on their work in a manner they would've dug.

The opening track on this CD is an Ernest Tubb tune titled "Kansas City Blues." You can hear the band slappin' and pickin' and soloin' like mad. It's a good song not because it's a "retro" carbon copy of Tubb's sound, but because it's a natural perpetuation of his style.

"Drive on" is one of the most spectacular road songs ever recorded. Listen to it a couple times and tell me it's not the perfect tune to have in your car stereo the next time you take Highway 10 to Los Angeles. It's also a salute of sorts to the legacy of the country musicians who traveled the same roads over and over long ago. "Wild Free & Reckless" is an ode to wandering in the same vein as Hancock's "Thunderstorms and Neon Signs." Lyrically he's got that middle 20th century travel aesthetic pegged better than anybody else I've ever heard. "It's Saturday Night", "Gone Gone Gone" and "Gonna be Some Trouble Tonight" are all jolly, rowdy numbers that have one foot planted in hickified rockabilly and the other in the primordial ooze of eternal Texas juke joint leg shakin' music.

The CD ends on a quiet note with "You Don't Have to Cry" with a completely different melancholy sound dating back to when Grandma (or maybe even her ma) was young.

This mellow, citified jazz style seems to be another of Wayne's obsessions. Hubba hubba.

17. EPILOGUE

Well, what do you think? Is anybody still there? I don't expect anyone to agree with all of my musical choices, since as I pointed out in the introduction music is just a matter of opinion. I'm very hopeful you enjoyed reading most of this book and will seek out recordings by the artists I've tried my best to put over.

Even though I've received review copies for other magazine articles and reviews, I paid for 100% of the albums and CDs you've just read about. There's no collusion at work behind the scenes even though I've met some of these folks.

It's a fact that if I had an unlimited budget, or hell, any sort of budget to work with I would've included releases by folks like the Delmore Brothers, the Louvins and Kay Adams. I have scores of Johnny Cash records, but no funds to buy the dozens I don't have for consideration in a book. I'm damn proud of the section about obscure singers, but am all too aware that I could have filled this book twice over with rare stuff just as good if I had unlimited $$$ to work with. Oh well, at least I don't owe any money on the albums I do own.

I've written a few other books in my time and a heap of reviews and columns, but nothing like this. I began working on this in 2003 and gave up on it for a couple of years figuring it wouldn't see the light of day. It was originally going to be the "Best 245 Real Country Albums of all Time," or something like that. I spent months lining the releases up in order of quality in my humble opinion. I'm intending to post at my website a listing of at least the top 100 or so in the order I originally intended.

I encountered some problems during what was meant to be a brief stopping point I used to send out some book proposals. First off, I went back to finish off my college degree. I learned enough writing papers for my history professors (my major) and in a creative writing class (for my English minor) to realize that the punctuation I originally used to write this book was off the charts crude.

Another problem was due to the fact that I learned a great deal about country music history in the course at the university I mentioned in the introduction. It wasn't that I didn't know what I was writing about in the first edition of this book, it was just that I learned so much more, I knew I'd be re-writing the damn thing.

I rewrote the reviews during breaks from school. Even though I received some rejections from a few publishers, I never heard back from the book outfit in Nashville that was the most clearly devoted to country music. Was my submission with a stamped return envelope lost in the mail?

Or did they hate my book so much they didn't even dignify it with a response? I really wanted to know badly enough that I sent another proposal letter and then another a few months after that.

How sad. I never got a word back from the publisher I targeted as perfect for this book. See; I was rejected by Nashville too. Oh, the shame!

I never intended this book to be anything but an honest statement of my opinions about country music. I'm used to writing for rock/metal/punk audiences in various magazines that recruit me specifically because I don't mince words when I feel it's necessary to attack a sacred icon from the rock music world. I'm not quite sure whether it's my words and theory about Poco and the Eagles or Saint Parsons that was so offensive, or perhaps something else I haven't considered.

I'm sure as hell not going to ever sanitize mean words from a book that clearly is meant to state my opinion. If you think I've been brutal or over the top, consider all of the attacks over the years from salaried mainstream critics slagging country stalwarts as dumb rednecks.

I tabled the project for a couple whole years figuring it'd never see the light of day. Oddly enough, I kept getting requests from long-term readers eager to read the book. A double handful of persistent people never let up. I considered sticking it for free on my diary website, even made a written promise to.

In the end the birth of my first grandson Hank, here in 2011, inspired me to smash a drinking table with my fist and determine the book had to see the light of day; in case anything happens to me, how will he know what country music to listen to?

That's the story of the book. Are there any questions?

What's that? Why is there no Ronnie Milsap or Alabama or Dan Seals covered in this book? I guess I have one more group of music fans to piss off.

In the '80's, as many of the artists I've worshipped in this book were receiving pink slips, there was a trend towards mushy, heavily produced slow songs by both a crop of new recruits and pop artists as well. I have very little patience for this stuff. You will find with very little search effort on the internet hordes of people who hated the "country lite" music from this era.

I have a special sub genre name for it: "S.O.B. country" which stands for "Sappy Overwrought Ballads."

The following is a hastily concocted list of several of my least favorite songs of the '70's and '80's. Hopefully this listing will answer any remaining questions some readers may still have as to what makes me tick. Some of these graced the country charts and others stunk up the pop top 40. Some of them are S.O.B. tunes and others just irk me.

"Wild Fire" Michael Murphy, "Have You Never Been Mellow" Olivia Newton John, "Sometimes When We Touch" Dan Hill, "We Built This City" Starship, "Muskrat Love" Captain and Tennile, "New Kid In Town" Eagles, "Feelings" Morris Albert, "Shannon" Henry Gross, "Tin Man" America, "The Logical Song" Supertramp, "Elvira" Oak Ridge Boys, "If" Bread, "It's Still Rock and Roll to Me" Billy Joel, "Let Your Love Flow" Bellamy Brothers.

There's one more type of country that you might have expected to see in these pages. Some people get really nervous right off the bat when they see somebody walking down the street or drinking at a bar packing a weapon.

I myself get similarly uneasy when I see individuals of either sex perched on a stool with an acoustic guitar. Yes, I'm aware of the fact that hundreds of songs on the releases I've just written about were composed by and in some cases performed by singers backed by just their guitar.

I'm suspicious by nature of singer songwriter albums. Hank Sr. and Johnny Cash and Waylon and scores of others can keep it interesting with just their guitar, voice and stories. From coast to coast there are thousands of "sensitive" souls who torture their fellow human beings with, tedious, boring relationship songs. The singer songwriters serve a great need behind the scenes, but their entertainment factor is often nil.

Blowhards who fantasize they're really baring their souls and thusly "touching" us are out there in vast numbers. My wife and I made a pact early in our marriage to never, ever leave guitars out where folks can get to them.

Keep those cards and letters coming.

Phil Irwin

P.O. Box 1781

San Marcos, TX 78666

whiskeyrebel@whiskeyrebel.com

BIBLIOGRAPHY

Emery, Ralph MEMORIES (1991 Scribner).

Coe, David Allan JUST FOR THE RECORD (1978 self published).

Tucker, Tanya NICKEL DREAMS (1998 Hyperion).

Porterfeld, Nolan JIMMIE RODGERS: LIFE AND TIMES (1979 University of Illinois Press).

Parton, Dolly DOLLY: MY LIFE AND OTHER UNFINISHED BUSINESS (1994 Harper Collins).

Schiff, Ronny BOB WILLS: KING OF WESTERN SWING (1997 Hal Leonard).

Wald, Elijah HOW THE BEATLES DESTROYED ROCK N ROLL: AN ALTERNATE HISTORY (2009 Oxford University Press, USA).

Nelson, Willie, Shrake, Bud WILLIE: AN AUTOBIOGRAPHY (1998 Simon & Schuster).

Barger, Sonny RIDIN' HIGH, LIVIN' FREE (2003 Harper Collins).

Logan, Horace ELVIS, HANK AND ME (1998 St. Martins).

Escott, Colin TATTOOED ON THEIR TONGUES (1996 Music Sales Corp).

Swenson, John BILL HALEY THE DADDY OF ROCK AND ROLL (1983 Scarborough).

Guralnick, Peter CARELESS LOVE (1999 Little, Brown).

Guralnick, Peter LAST TRAIN TO MEMPHIS (1999 Little, Brown).

Eng, Steven A SATISFIED MIND (1992 Rutledge Hill).

Faragher, Scott MUSIC CITY BABYLON (1992 Birch Lane).

Escott, Colin HANK WILLIAMS THE BIOGRAPHY (1994 Little, Brown).

Paris, Mike, Comber, Chris JIMMIE THE KID (1975 Da Capo).

Escott, Colin GOOD ROCKIN' TONIGHT SUN RECORDS AND THE BIRTH OF ROCK AND ROLL (1980 Quick Fox).

Tosches, Nick COUNTRY: THE TWISTED ROOTS OF ROCK AND ROLL (1977 Da Capo).

Tosches, Nick HELLFIRE: THE JERRY LEE LEWIS STORY (1982 Grove Press).

Malone, Bill COUNTRY MUSIC USA (2002 University of Texas Press).

Lewis, Linda Gail THE DEVIL, ME, AND JERRY LEE (1998 Longstreet).

Cooper, Daniel LEFTY FRIZZELL: THE HONKY TONK LIFE OF COUNTRY MUSICS GREATEST SINGER (1995 Little, Brown).

Pugh, Ronnie ERNEST TUBB: THE TEXAS TROUBADOR (1996 Duke Press).

Jennings, Waylon WAYLON AN AUTOBIOGRAPHY (1996 Warner Books).

Cash Johnny CASH: THE AUTOBIOGRAPHY (1997 Harper).

Jones, George I LIVED TO TELL IT ALL (1996 Villard Books).

Tosches, Nick WHERE DEAD VOICES GATHER (2001 Little, Brown).

Haslam, Gerald WORKIN' MAN BLUES: COUNTRY MUSIC IN CALIFORNIA (University of California Press).

Zwonitzer, Mark WILL YOU MISS ME WHEN I'M GONE: THE CARTER FAMILY AND THEIR LEGACY IN AMERICAN MUSIC (2002 Simon & Schuster).

Bush, Johnny WHISKEY RIVER TAKE MY MIND (2007 University of Texas Press).

Lynn, Loretta STILL WOMAN ENOUGH (2002 Hyperion Books).

Escott, Colin HANK WILLIAMS: SNAPSHOTS FROM THE LOST HIGHWAY (2001 Da Capo Press).

Haggard, Merle SING ME BACK HOME (1983 Pocket).

Amburn, Ellis DARK STAR THE ROY ORBISON STORY (1991 New English Library).

Jones, Louis M. (Grandpa) FIFTY YEARS BEHIND THE MIKE (1984 University of Tennessee).

Smith, Richard CAN'T YOU HEAR ME CALLING: THE STORY OF BILL MONROE, THE FATHER OF BLUE GRASS (2000 Little Brown)

ABOUT THE AUTHOR

Phil Irwin (aka The Whiskey Rebel) has entertained readers across the country and around the world with columns and reviews in music and art magazines; including Carbon 14, Hit List and Amp.

In 2001, he launched a frequently updated Internet diary (www.whiskeyrebel.com). This is his fourth book. He is a veteran musician and a competitive chess player.

In 2008, the author received a baccalaureate degree in History (with an English minor) from Texas State University. He graduated cum laude was twice honored with The Achievement in History Award.

Phil currently lives in San Marcos, Texas with his wife Marla, and two loyal cats: Dixie and Nutty.

Other books by Phil Irwin
Jobjumper
Hostile City or Bust
Escape from Cookieland

www.ingramcontent.com/pod-product-compliance
Lightning Source LLC
LaVergne TN
LVHW051623080426
835511LV00016B/2144
9780615535647